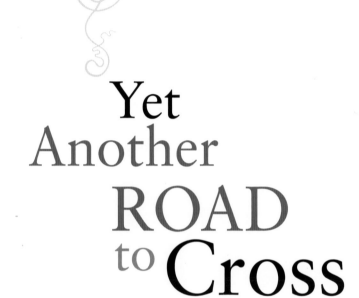

Yet Another ROAD to Cross

TEN GENERATIONS OF THE CARRAU FAMILY IN WINE
1752 - 2012

Yet Another Road to Cross
TEN GENERATIONS OF THE CARRAU FAMILY IN WINE
1752-2012
CHRISTOPHER FIELDEN

© 2012, Vinos Finos Juan Carrau S.A.
© 2012, Christopher Fielden
© 2012, Montevideo - Uruguay

Edited in spanish by Random House Mondadori
Title. In Vino Veritas, La Familia Carrau y el Vino

Editor: Margarita Carrau
Editors Consulting: Francisco Carrau and Javier Carrau
Correction: Lys Hall
Design: Bettina Díaz
Cover Picture: By Carlos Contrera, Cerro Chapeu view (Rivera)
Photographs and documents from the files of Bodegas Carrau
First edition published January 2013

Printed by IMPRIMEX S.A
Depósito Legal 395.014

www. bodegascarrau.com
info@bodegascarrau.com

ISBN: 978-9974-98-983-2

"With thanks to all the family for their thoughts and memories."

Christopher

INTRODUCTION

Some times when you write a book, you begin with a title and then write to it. With this book, however, inspiration was some time in coming as far as the title was concerned. We sat round a table and came up with a number of suggestions. These we cut down to three and asked a number of friends for their reactions. Not one person was in favour of *Yet Another Road to Cross*. I will begin, therefore, by explaining why it was chosen.

This book is the story of one family's life in wine, over ten generations and in three countries; that accounts for the sub-title. However, the story is not a simple one. Over the years, the family moved on, it faced challenges. It moved from a small village in Catalunya to a developing city in Uruguay. It crossed the Atlantic Ocean from Europe to South America. On arriving there, it has not remained quietly in one place. On two occasions it has made a leap forward by literally crossing the road; firstly when Juan Carrau Pujol decided that his future lay not with Santa Rosa at César Mayo Gutierrez 2211, Colón, but rather at César Mayo Gutierrez 2556, at an even number, rather than an odd one! More recently, the establishment of a vineyard and winery in the Campanha region of Brazil has meant that the only two things that separate that property from the Cerro Chapeu estate in Uruguay are the frontier and a road.

There is something about crossing a road that implies both moving forward and also taking a risk. On reading this book, I hope that you will see that, over the generations, the Carraus have steadily moved forward, though with what might appear to be an occasional small step backwards.

They have also been prepared to take risks; some of their ventures have been on the gargantuan scale.

I have said that this is a family story and here I must offer an apology. Whilst this book should have been written at arm's length, it is a story in which I have been peripherally involved for more than twenty years, from the moment I first met Javier Carrau Bonomi at a trade fair in Cologne. Because of this you will find that the narrative occasionally lapses into the first person.

As this story takes place over a number of centuries in three countries there may appear a variety of spellings of places and names. Thus I have come across four different ways of spelling Vilassar, the village where, time-wise, most of the story takes place. I have found it spelt variously with one or two l's and with one or two s's. I have tried to stick to one l and two s's, except when I am quoting someone directly, it might appear differently.

Yet again a Pau in Catalan is a Pablo in Uruguay and a Joan turns into a Juan. With regard to surnames the Catalan Juan Carrau i Sust in South America becomes Juan Carrau Sust. Here I have tried to respect the continental differences.

I have found the lives of successive Carraus, and the wines that the current generation produces, fascinating.

I hope you do too.

Christopher Fielden
November 2011.

THANKS.

My thanks are firstly due to the current generation of the Carrau family for their help and advice in assembling the material for this book. It is also fortunate that there are four separate sources for the background to the family. Firstly there is the registry of the church of San Juan in Vilassar. Here are recorded, almost from its construction in the first half of the eighteenth century, all the births, marriages and deaths that took place in the village. Secondly, Juan Carrau Sust prepared, for the baptism of his first son, Juan Carrau Pujol in March 1924, a detailed family tree going back to the end of the seventeenth century. Also, when he finally emigrated to Uruguay in 1929, he brought with him a great deal of material about the family. Finally there is the diary of Juan Carrau Ferrés, which records, in minute detail, his life when he arrived in Montevideo in 1843, even down to what he had for lunch each day. All these contribute pieces that is the jigsaw that goes to make up the story of the Carrau family in wine.

In addition, I would particularly like to thank:

in Vilassar:

Joan Giménez i Blasco: schoolteacher and historian, who showed me around Vilassar and made the initial contacts for me.

Isabel Ayala of the Biblioteca Municipal Ernest Lluch, who sought out source books for me.

Joaquim Carrau García, cartoonist and hairdresser, who gave leads to family connections.

Josep M. Carrau, economist, who also gave details of the Carrau diaspora and researched the origins of the name.

In Montevideo:

Dra. Matilde Carrau, Director of Carrau y Cía., S.A., who kindly provided information from the family and company archives.

Daniel Mutio, Director of Bodegas y Viñedos Santa Rosa, who gave his memories of the company's connection with the Carrau family.

Finally I would like to thank Lys Hall for checking the text for me and my wife for her support.

CHAPTER I

In the beginning......
Vilassar de Mar.

Every history is like a play; it has its acts and its scenes, it has its cast of characters and it has its time when it takes place. For this play, the cast of characters is clear; it is led by the members of the Carrau family over a number of generations. Where the acts take place is also clear; firstly in Vilassar de Mar, then in Uruguay and Brazil. What is not so clear is the time when the first scene actually takes place.

Vilassar de Mar is now largely a dormitory town for Barcelona, lying some fifteen miles along the coast to the north-east of the city and joined to it umbilically by the N11 main road and the railway line. Historically, it has been linked to the sea, though since the middle of the eighteenth century it has been known, firstly for its wines, then for the production of Mataró Royal potatoes, with Britain being the largest market, and more recently for its flowers, produced in an ocean of greenhouses. When our story starts, its population was very close to zero; now it is approaching twenty thousand, many living in modern high-rise blocks of apartments.

The distant history of the Carrau family is not recorded. Certainly the name would suggest that that their origins were in France and it seems that in medieval Gascon the word *carrau* was used as term for a mixture of cereals, though apparently in modern Catalan slang it is the word for a football rattle! Juan Carrau Sust, in the family tree he created, also suggests that it origins might suggest the family's origins as quarrymen.

The first mention of a Carrau in Vilassar is of Juan Carrau, who married a Margarita Strany in 1651, though in a provincial census of 1640 the surname does appear elsewhere. If his origins are French, there are two feasible alternatives as to why he had arrived in Catalunya at that time, both of them relating to the widespread political turbulence in Europe then present. This was the time of the War of the Spanish Succession and both in France and Spain the governments were having difficulty in financing their army. In both cases, the main burden of the extra taxes imposed fell upon the lower classes. This led to peasants' revolts in the two countries: in France, particularly in the south-west, in Gascony, beginning in 1635, by various bands of rebels, who collectively came to be known as the *croquants*. It might be that the Carraus went into exile, as a result of this.

An alternative possibility could be because of the revolution in Catalunya from 1640 to 1653 against the overwhelming increase of taxes there. This was known as *La Guerra de Segadors* and, in 1650, King Louis XIV of France sent troops to relieve the Spanish rebels who were being besieged in Barcelona by Spanish government forces under the command of the Duke of Albuquerque. Might Juan, or Jean, Carrau have been part of that French army? It was not uncommon for local girls to marry French soldiers, though Juan (or Joan) is described in the marriage registry as being a fisherman and not a native of Vilassar. A son, the first of five and two daughters, was born just a few days after the wedding – again not a rare occurrence in those days.

This wedding would not have taken place in the records of Vilassar de Mar, for in those days it scarcely existed, but rather in the church of St. Genís, at Vilasar d'Alt, some six and a half kilometres away up in the hills. Living by the sea was perceived to be too dangerous as one was at the mercy of the many raids that used to be made by corsairs from North Africa who used to ravage the Mediterranean seaboard. Indeed such was the fear of pillaging that three towers were built on the shore-line, in which the fishermen might take refuge. Only one of these towers still remains,

La Torre d'en Nadal – once the property of Josefa Carrau Sust.

La Torre d'en Nadal built at the end of the fifteenth century. This was later to belong to Josefa Carrau Sust, the sister of Juan Carrau Sust, who emigrated to Uruguay in 1930.

With the increase in naval strength of the European powers, the influence of the pirates diminished and was finally eliminated by a specific campaign against them in 1785 by King Carlos III. As a result Vilassar de Mar was able to establish itself as a community in its own right. In 1723 it was recorded as having no more than twenty-three houses, but the community petitioned for a church to be built to satisfy its spiritual needs. (One of the five family names mentioned in this petition is that of Carrau.) Following this the church, dedicated to John the Baptist, was built, but this cannot have been a totally satisfactory solution, for fifteen years later, there was a further request for a priest to say the mass on Sundays and Feast days. By 1770, the number of houses had increased to 180, though a map of that time shows there being just one street, with the church at the end of it.

From the end of the seventeenth century agriculture had come to the fertile plain behind the village, which until then had been covered with dense forests. The fishermen, whose season largely began with the catching of sardines, from St. Michael's day, at the end of September, onwards, began to diversify, planting orange and lemon trees. Sadly these suffered seriously from frosts and they then took to planting vineyards, as an additional way of boosting their income. (There were already extensive vineyards in Vilassar d'Alt, from where the Bosch family sold wine on the market of Barcelona.)

The first mention that we have of a member of the Carrau family producing wine comes in the inventory of a certain Pau Carrau in 1730. He was a great-grandson of the original Juan Carrau and is also described as a fisherman. However, he also owned one plot of vines next to his house and another one adjoining those of the Marqués de Moja, the Lord of Vilassar Castle. His cellar is also listed as holding eight barrels and it is not difficult to envisage that these might be full of wine.

However our story does not really begin with Pau Carrau, but rather with one of his cousins, Francisco Carrau, also a fisherman, who on April 2nd 1752 bought "all that piece of land planted in vines of three hundred and forty-four *cuarteras* situated within the boundary of the said Parish of Vilassar on the land named El Emparrado de Casals, that was sold by Ramón Casanovas to Francisco Carrau for the price of five *centavos*, seventy-one *sueldos*

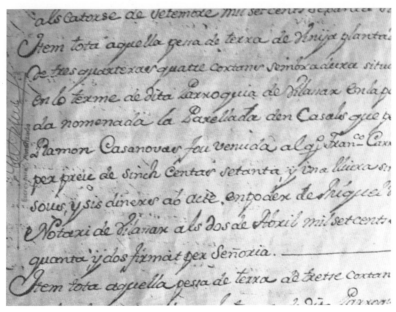

Part of the deed of sale of the vineyard purchased by Francisco Carrau Vehils in 1752.

and six *dineros*." (An *emparrado* is a vine that has been trained to a stake.)

In Catalunya the tradition was that the oldest son should take on responsibility for the property, whilst younger sons had to make their own way in the world. Francisco Carrau Vehils, in due course, passed his wine interests on to his son, Francisco Carrau Mir, though the latter died in 1775, whilst his father lived a further eight years. The grandson, Lorenzo Carrau Girbau then inherited the business. He died in 1810 and was succeeded by his oldest son Francisco Carrau Amat. He was only twenty years old at the time, but was to live for a further fifty years, a period of dramatic change in the nature of the village. This Francisco is credited with having planted the noble grape varieties, Monastrell and Garnacha, in his vineyards in about 1810

During these years, Vilassar de Mar seems to have taken on new importance, probably at the expense of its mother village in the hills. Whilst there is little information on the wine-trade during this time, the Carrau family appears to have played an ever-increasing role in this expansion. As early as 1764, Jaume Carrau Mir, the brother of the younger Francisco, was involved in purchasing land for the construction of the new street of St. Andreu and sixty years later, Lorenzo's sister Magí, was investing in a further street – coincidentally named St. Magí. In 1822, two members of the family are recorded as having contributed to the war fighting fund and in 1849, Francisco was well enough established in wines to have purchased a *bodega*, or warehouse.

At the end of the eighteenth century and the beginning of the nineteenth, Vilassar was still primarily a fishing village. In 1773, a mutual society was formed to look after the families of those fishermen lost at sea and as late as

1836 half of the heads of families still claimed to earn their living from fishing.

By the middle of the nineteenth century however, there appears to have been a dramatic change and the first really detailed description we have of Vilassar comes in a work by Pascual Madoz, written in 1850, and quoted by Joan Giménez i Blasco in his book *De la Vela al Vapor*. By then the village had developed into a town, boasting five hundred houses, a population of almost two thousand, a town hall and a primary school with four hundred pupils. "The soil is sandy and of medium quality….. It produces poor wheat and maize, wine, barley, beans, vegetables and oranges, enough cattle to see to the ploughing, and also there is fishing." It seems from this as though the production of wine was in no way predominant in local life. This becomes even more apparent when he continues, "As for industry, there are three factories producing cotton thread, ten for weaving, with 211 steam-driven looms, lace-producers, two flour mills, fishing, which has a fleet of fifteen boats, employing seventy people and shipbuilding." This last had, over the previous twenty years had produced more than 260 boats ranging in size from a frigate down to fishing smacks. More important however to our story is "Moreover, there are fifteen boats, which are constantly voyaging to America…" It is this part of Vilassar's life that is to prove essential to the future of the Carrau family. Within the next decade, trade with the Americas had grown to such an extent that fifty local ships were involved in it and by 1880 the number had grown to seventy-five.

The importance of seafaring to the community can also be judged by two of the most important buildings in the town, both constructed about this time. The first is the *casino*, or club, of captains and pilots, with its façade on

The Monjo Nautical School 1876.

The classes of 1892 and 1893 with members of staff.

one side of the main square. This was built in 1845 and the second, even more imposing edifice, is the Escuela Monjo de Náutica, or marine training school, established in 1876, to which children were sent as young as eleven years old on a three year course. From this, they would graduate as assistant pilots. This basic qualification led to the better students becoming captains by the age of thirty.

At the time there were 265 hectares of vineyards in the village, with exports of wine already being made to the Americas. No doubt much of the production was also sent to the neighbouring town of Mataró, which had become a major centre for the distillation of brandy, again a potential product for export. The vines suffered, as they did elsewhere in Europe, from the onset of *oïdium*, or powdery mildew, in 1858. By then the treatment for this, dusting with sulphur, had already been discovered in France, so it did not prove to be a major problem.

More serious was the arrival of *phylloxera* in 1886. In the short term this created increased markets for the wines of Catalunya, as the disease had reached France some twenty years before, leading firstly to demand for wine from that country and secondly to the investment by French wine companies in Spain, particularly in Rioja and Catalunya. Interestingly it was two local pharmacists, Castellet and Almera, who were at the forefront of the fight against *phylloxera* in Spain. The latter actually lived and worked in Vilassar.

It is perhaps surprising that the author makes no mention of the railway that arrived in the town in 1846, for this was the first line on mainland Spain, linking Barcelona to Mataró. (Mainland Spain, because it seems that a railway had already been built in Cuba, which then formed part of Spain.) The arrival of this line reduced the travelling

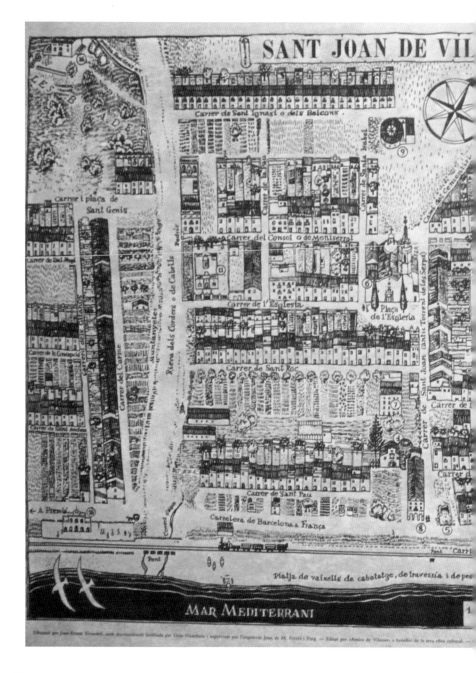

SANT JOAN DE VIL

LES BOADES

Carrer de Sant Ignasi o dels Balcons.

Carrer i plaça de Sant Genís

Carrer del Consol o de Montserrat

Carrer de l'Església

Plaça de l'Església

Carrer del Carme

Carrer de Sant Roc

Carrer de Sant Pau

Carretera de Barcelona a França

← A Premià

Platja de vaixells de cabotatge, de travessia i de pes

MAR MEDITERRANI

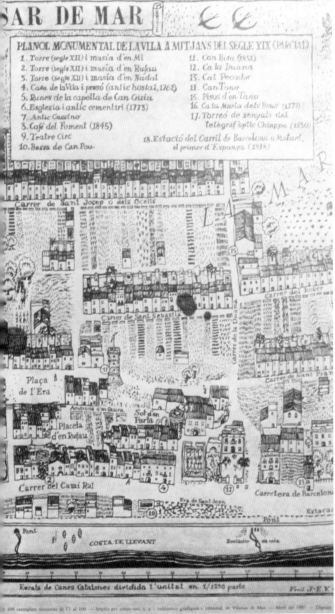

SAR DE MAR

PLANOL MONUMENTAL DE LA VILA A MITJANS DEL SEGLE XIX (PARCIAL)

1. Torre (segle XII) i masia d'en Mi
2. Torre (segle XII) i masia d'en Rufau
3. Torre (segle XII) i masia d'en Nadal
4. Casa de la Vila i presó (antic hostal, 1762)
5. Runes de la capella de Can Guiu
6. Esglesia i antic cementiri (1773)
7. Antic Cassino
8. Cafè del Foment (1845)
9. Teatre Circ
10. Bassa de Can Pou

11. Can Bisa (1851)
12. Ca la Iuana
13. Cal Pecador
14. Can Tano
15. Pisos d'en Tano
16. Ca la Maria dels Bous (1773)
17. Torreó de senyals del Telègraf òptic Chiappa (1850)

18. Estació del Carril de Barcelona a Mataró, el primer d'Espanya (1848)

Carrer de Sant Josep o dels Ocells

Carrer del Roser

Carrer de Sant Sebastià

Carrer de la Duana

Plaça de l'Era

Androna d'en Saura

Sot d'en Parla

Carrer de Sant Fran

Placeta d'en Rufau

Carrer del Camí Ral

Era de Sant Joan

Carretera de Barcelon

Estaci

Pont

COSTA DE LLEVANT

Pont

LA MAR

Escala de Canes Catalanes dividida l'unitat en 1/1250 parts

Fecit J. E. V.

A map of Vilassar drawn in the middle of the 19th century by Joan-Ernest Vinardell Note the recently constructed railway-line towards the bottom of the map.

time from Barcelona from five hours to less than an hour and this must have made an important impact on the future development of the town. It also lowered the cost of distribution of local products.

The ships owners and captains were the new aristocracy of the town, building ornate houses on the sea-front, the Carrer St. Pau. One has on its façade a *porrón*, the traditional Catalan wine jug and a gourd for *mate*, the drink of Uruguay, symbolising the links between the two countries. The traders and budding industrialists had to be content with owning houses one, or more, streets back.

At this stage in the story, we come to a major diversion on the route. Juan Carrau Ferrés was born in Vilassar in 1823. At a very young age he became an apprentice in one of the local textile mills, which he described as being "as bad a hell as one could speak of." He then went to work in another mill where he was promoted to being a clerk. When he was still only thirteen, his uncle Antonio upbraided him for having no ambition and had him join the crew of his own ship. On his first voyage the seas were so rough that he was unable to eat for three days. Despite this early discomfort, he continued and, at the age of sixteen, he qualified as a junior pilot after attending a course at the marine college in Mataró.

He then made a short voyage on the ketch *Marcial* and returned from Málaga to Barcelona with a cargo of wine. On February 16th 1840, he set sail from Barcelona on the *Orestes* for Puerto Rico, La Guayra and the island of Trinidad. He followed this up with a voyage to Havana leaving Santander on Christmas Day of the same year. On his return, he had just a month's leave on shore before transferring to another brigantine the *Místico Mercurio*, as second pilot, leaving Barcelona for Murcia and South America.

As we have seen, there was already an important merchant fleet, based in Vilassar, but generally sailing from Barcelona, to trade in the Americas. The initial cargo would be of wine and brandy, which would be off-loaded, after a voyage of over forty days in a port on the River Plate, most commonly Montevideo. From there hides and beef would be shipped either to Havana, in Cuba, to be exchanged for sugar and rum, or to New Orleans or Charleston, for cotton, for the European markets. This transatlantic expansion came to be called *La Aventura Catalana* – The Catalan Adventure.

Some idea of how important the transatlantic trade had become can be gained from studying the marine career of one of the captains, Feliciá Sust Cisa. In the twenty-one years from 1831, he made twenty-six voyages to the Americas; his most regular route being from Barcelona to Havana to New Orleans and home. His son, Jaume Sust Alsina over a career from 1855 to 1898, sailed regularly on voyages, some almost two years long, to Montevideo, up the Uruguay River to Paysandu, Havana and back again. His sister married another sea-captain, a member of the Carrau family.

These voyages were largely financed by shore-based investors, who might take a part-share either in the ship, or in its succession of cargoes. Thus the economy of Vilassar came to be largely dependent on marine trade.

The voyage of the *Místico Mercurio* was to be ill-fated. During a violent storm on January 5th 1841, Juan fell out, as did most of the crew, with the boatswain. So heated was the dispute that when the boat docked in Montevideo, he decided to jump ship. There he was in a country where he knew nobody and with no money – and just seventeen years old. The first Carrau had come to settle in Uruguay.

He left his bags with a certain Jaime Tremoleras and found a job as a messenger boy with company called Castells. He must have been a hard worker because in a short time he was promoted to being captain of a frigate that they owned, that used to sail up the Uruguay River to purchase tobacco and *mate*. The condition of the ship cannot have been good for it was soon destined for the shipbreaker's yard.

With the money he earned, he and Jaime Tremoleras bought a general store for 900 *pesos*. They soon discovered that their purchase was ill-advised for it was outside the city in an area of washerwomen and carters and its real value was no more than 200 *pesos*. Despite all this, they pulled the building down and rebuilt a new room five metres deep and ten metres wide. At the back they built a warehouse a metre and a half deep and also installed a mezzanine floor, which was reached by a stairway of soap-boxes.

Life must have been difficult at the start, for daily takings were regularly under 5 *pesos*. Juan was meticulous in keeping a diary, in which he recorded the minutiae of

La pulpería que fundara en 1843 don Juan Carrau —superando las vicisitude zozobra histórica— se transformó 25 años después en un almacén por mayor nombre de "Carrau y Cía.". Esta sencilla estampa habla bien claro de lo qu que ha conquistado tal éxito en el comercio de hoy.

Contemporary sketch of "La Nave" – The Ship store.

daily life. He must have been relieved when he was able to write, "I remember that one day when we managed to take twelve *pesos*, we were as happy as sandboys."

Salvation came from a most unlikely source: soap! One day, they were called upon by a salesman, Sandalio González, who offered them a locally produced soap. They were not at all keen on taking this on, but he insisted, saying there was a ready market on their doorstep, the community of washerwomen. This proved to be the case and "Within a month, sales of soap had gone mad and we were selling as much as seventy *pesos'* worth a day; we were able to build up considerable savings." A short time afterwards, he could say with confidence, "With good wine, good *yerba (mate)* good oil and good soap the business cannot fail." He was proud to name his business "The Ship", and write beneath the title on the store-front the three words "Honesty and Probity."

The partnership with Sr. Tremoleras did not last and was officially dissolved on September 25th, 1844, but the latter could always be called upon in the future to finance a special purchase when necessary. Juan Carrau spent much of his time at the quayside, talking to the ships' captains, many of whom would have been relatives and friends from Vilassar. He also used to dine on board regularly. No doubt he had some nostalgia for the food of his native Catalunya.

A typical entry in his diary is that for August 13th, 1851, "As we were walking along the wharf, we met a Catalan who said he was called Joaquín Turra. He asked if I was a grandson of Pablo Ferrés. I replied that I was and he said that he had sailed twice on the schooner belonging to Sr. Mirambell, when Pablo Ferrés was pilot and my brother Lorenzo assistant pilot and that he thought highly of the

Juan Carrau Ferrés

two of them." In such a way he maintained close contact with home, as well as, one imagines, building up a substantial business as a ship's chandler.

In 1856, Juan's elder brother Lorenzo died, not long after his marriage, at the age of thirty-five, so Juan, now the oldest surviving son, returned to Spain to take up his family responsibilities. However he left the increasingly profitable company in Montevideo in the hands of his brother Pablo and cousin Pedro, with the name of the company changing to Carrau Hermanos in 1857. Another brother José, was also based in Montevideo, sailing to the various ports up to Uruguay River, distributing goods to the local merchants,

A stock sheet from just two years later shows that drink had become an important part of their business, for it includes 48 demijohns of gin, 33 demijohns of *anís de Majorca*, 47 cases of French *vin ordinaire*, a barrel of

Malaga, two barrels of dark beer, as well as Champagne and Frontignan. More local products were *yerba mate* and cigars from Paraguay. By 1864, the company also owned its own ship, the *Corinne*, which enabled them to become exporters as well as importers.

(The tradition of the Carrau family in the spirits trade continues to this day. For many years they were the distributors in Uruguay of the Diageo range of products, though now they represent the Campari Group. They were also producers of the leading brand of 'domestic' whisky *Old Times.*)

From such humble beginnings was born what is now called Carrau y Cia. S.A., one of the most powerful agency and distribution companies in Uruguay; a company which is still owned entirely by the Carrau family. More importantly for our story, however, it provided a solid point of contact, in the future, in the country, for any adventurous member from the Spanish side of the family. How important this became to the Carraus of our story will be seen on more than one occasion.

There was much coming and going between the two branches of the family in Montevideo and Vilassar. For example, Juan's brother Pablo married Micaela Trujillo in Montevideo, but after she had died, and he had made his fortune, he returned to Vilassar, where he married again and settled down.

The third of the three original family partners, the cousin Pedro, was now the only one to remain in Montevideo. He had six sons of whom the youngest Francisco became a partner in 1908. It was planned that he should take over the running of the company, and he, together with his nephew, who was also his personal secretary, made a trip to Europe to visit their suppliers, including Juan Carrau

Sust in Vilassar. Sadly they took the decision to return to Uruguay via New York and, on the spur of the moment, booked tickets on the ill-fated voyage of the Titanic, where they both died on April 15th 1912. Among the family archives is a Cunard White Star card written by Francisco, posted when Titanic called in at Queenstown, Ireland.

Juan Carrau Ferrés took over control of the family vineyards in Vilassar in 1860 and married María Angela Mir Amat. It is recorded that by 1870, he was selling wine in the Americas. His eldest son, Francisco Carrau Mir, was born on December 23rd 1860. For him, life was particularly difficult as, at the age of eight, he had a serious fall from his horse, when out riding, and became deaf as a result. Where better to turn to for a new life but the New World and his cousins in Montevideo? At the age of fifteen, he sailed there on the *Savoie* with Bartolomé Casanovas, a distant cousin

The ketch Tuya, owned by the Carrau family and employed in shipping wine to the Americas.

1822 - 1897

D. Juan Carrau y Ferrés

Fundador de la marca "SAN Fco. JAVIER"

Piloto español de altura, comerciante destacado de Montevideo desde 1843 a 1857, fundador de la honorable firma "Carrau & Cia." de esta plaza, se dedicó más tarde a la exportación de vinos españoles radicándose en Vilasar de Mar (Barcelona); y difundió tan acreditados vinos en ambas orillas del Plata, que tenían que ser los precursores de los

que felizmente hemos logrado preparar aquí, con la misma marca de origen. Obtuvo medallas de oro en las Exposiciones Universales : Chicago 1893 y Barcelona 1888 cuyos altos premios le valieron entrar en las Antillas y en otros mercados de Centro América que fueron conquistados en breve espacio de tiempo para sus cuatro conocidas y acreditadas marcas:

"SAN Fco. JAVIER"
"BANDERA ESPAÑOLA"
"CALATAYUD"
"ESPADA"

Tribute to Juan Carrau Ferrés 1822-1897.

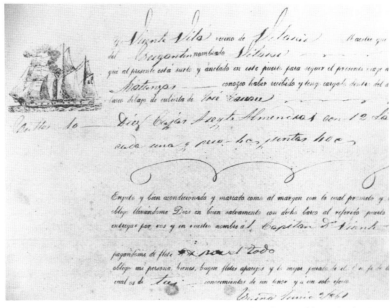

Bill of lading of the brigantine Vilassar, captain Vicente Vila, signed first officer, José Carrau Ferrés, the brother of Juan. September 1861.

and partner in Carrau Hermanos. (Coincidentally, it was a member of the Casanovas family that had originally sold to the Carrau family their vineyard a hundred and thirty years earlier.)

Francisco signed on as an apprentice to the Uruguayan Carraus, for four years at a monthly salary of 12 *pesos,* payable quarterly. He must have proved to be a success in this role for at the end of his apprenticeship he was given an eight per cent shareholding and a junior partnership in the company with a contract for a further four years. However, after only eight years in Uruguay he was called home by his father as his grandmother was seriously ill. Nevertheless, this did not prevent him from sailing to the River Plate on two further occasions in 1894 and 1902.

With his father, Francisco Carrau Mir seems to have breathed new life into the family holdings, at what must have been a difficult time in the wine-trade, though the family fortunes were probably aided by his marrying Rosa Sust, the daughter of Pau Sust Carrau, one of the leading shipowners in Vilassar. (Again, it is interesting to note how many cases there are of intermarriage between the same few families.)

Just nine years after his return to Vilassar, a balance sheet of his business shows just how diverse his interests were. Amongst the shareholders are listed the heirs of his aunt Maria Carrau Amat and Carrau y Cia. (Reciprocally, he was still a shareholder in the Montevideo company.) He owned houses and buildings valued at 78,000 *pesetas*, urban land, in Vilassar and Barcelona, worth 29,000 *pesetas*, wine valued at 111,501 *pesetas* and two-sevenths share in a boat

Francisco Carrau Mir

called the *Providencia*, not to mention shares in the cargoes on a number of boats. The original vineyard, La Mañana, purchased more than a century earlier was now in the books at 31,000 *pesetas*.

By now the family house was at 33, St. Sebastian Street and, just around the corner, there were two warehouses, where he stocked his wines. (One of these has now been converted into a dance studio, whilst the other is garages, with loft apartments above.)

It appears that he was no longer just selling the production of his own wines, but had become a general wine merchant selling both locally and overseas. In 1891, the records show that he shipped wine to Argentina, Venezuela, Brazil, Ecuador and Cuba. What wines was he selling? The most highly-priced wines listed were ones made from the Monastrell grape, as well as a wine called *Cielo*. (Could this be some form of Communion wine?) Also listed are Rancio, Priorato, Alicante, Macabeo, Garnacha and Torroja – this last, apparently, a wine from a sub-zone of Priorat.

In 1892, at the International Exhibition, held in Chicago to celebrate the four hundred years since the discovery of America by Columbus, Juan Carran (*sic*) of Vilasar de Mar, in Spain, was awarded a medal for his "Good Red Wine." Juan was to die four years later, aged seventy-four.

On his death, the company was trading as Hijos de Juan Carrau and its reputation was even more firmly established when a further gold medal was awarded to it, by *La Vanguardia*, then, and still now, Catalunya's leading daily newspaper. (It had been founded in 1881, largely to represent the views of the Catalan Liberal Party, but had since reshaped itself in a more independent mode.)

It was not in Francisco's nature to remain quietly in Vilassar looking after his wine interests, for he was a Carrau,

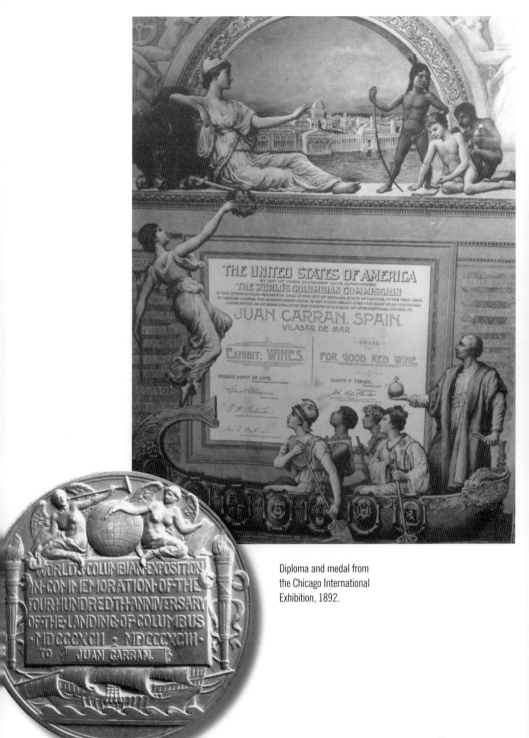

Diploma and medal from
the Chicago International
Exhibition, 1892.

perhaps the last, who considered the sea to be in his blood. He regularly sailed to the Americas and it was on one of these voyages, in 1902, to Ecuador, that he contracted pneumonia and died at the age of just forty-two.

Francisco, having qualified as a chemist in 1890, was also a technical man, for he patented a process for the removal of sulphites from wines prior to their distillation. Subsequent to his death, his widow continued trading for a further sixteen years under the title of "Viuda de Francisco Carrau" and the family archives contain a series of increasingly angry letters from E. Barbet, a Parisian company, boasting an office in Kiev, and a representative in the United States, which manufactured distillery equipment. Basically, these letters appear to dispute the validity of Francisco's patent within Spain. Sadly, no copies remain of the good widow's replies to them! One suspects that she may well have been the power behind the wine business. Though she retired in 1918, she lived for a further twenty years. It was only at the beginning of the Spanish Civil War that she left Vilassar for Montevideo and died there on November 27th 1938, at the age of seventy-one.

Juan Carrau Sust, our representative of the seventh generation of the family in wine, was born in 1890. He studied oenology at the wine school in Vilafranca del Penedés, where we get some idea of the daily timetable from an article he wrote some thirty years later. It was:

9a.m. – 10.30a.m Lectures: both theory and practice.

10.30a.m. – 11a.m. Methodical tasting of wines.

11a.m. – 1p.m. Analysis of wines, musts and *mistelas*.

3p.m. – 4.30p.m. Cellar work.

After 4.30p.m. Visits to *bodegas*.

Amongst these last visits he mentions the export cellars of Bosch Guell y Cia., the Solers estate of Eduardo

...sa Sust, widow of Francisco Carrau Mir, with children Francisco, Angelita, Juan and Josefa.

Survivors of the shipwreck off the coast of Florida, of the Rosa Alegret, which belonged to the Roig and Carrau families.

Maristanz, the *cava* cellars of Codorniu, in San Sadurni, the Can Bach estate and the Sindicato Vinícola of Pla de Penedés.

If we are to believe a local writer at about this period, it must have been a flourishing time for wine production in Vilassar for he writes that "the vineyards come down right to the beaches, descending in waves from the hillsides." However it cannot have lasted for it was then that the local flower industry began to expand. The arrival of electricity in the town made the pumping of water for irrigation much more practical.

Joanet Carrau Sust and Pau Roig, shareholders in the Rosa Alegret.

In Vilassar, Juan met and fell in love with Catalina Pujol, who lived in Montevideo, but was on a visit to Catalunya to see her relatives . (An F. Pujol is recorded as playing inside-left for the Vilassar football team, one of the first in Catalunya in 1912) When Juan sailed to Uruguay for the wedding, he brought with him a ring in which was inscribed the links over five generations by which their families were joined. He must have been a true romantic, because he also brought with him as gifts a pair of ear-rings, and a portrait of his bride-to-be that he had painted, showing her wearing those ear-rings!

Juan Carrau Sust.

For the christening of their first son, Juan Francisco Jaime Carrau Pujol, who was born in Barcelona on March 13th 1924, he constructed an elaborate, horizontal, family-tree. Dedicating it to his wife, he writes, in florid style, " Stimulated by the example of my august forefather, to whom I owe the source for my work, and also to commemorate the birth of this first male heir with which God has blessed our wedding, I have set about this simple work, with its uniquely family flavour, as the duty of an oldest son, that I want to dedicate to you: for me a small task, but at the same time large, for it comprises three centuries of honourable succession."

Christening gift of the Carrau family tree.

Portrait of Catalina Pujol, painted by Juan Carrau.

Wedding photo of Juan Carrau and Catalina Pujol in 1921.

Catalina and baby in arms 'Quico'.

The beginning of the twentieth century was a lively time in Catalan history. After Spain's defeat and final loss of its colonies in the Spanish-American War of 1898, (Uruguay had gained its independence in 1825) there grew up a powerful movement for independence, not just in Catalunya but also in the Basque country.

In addition the region began to flex its muscles as the industrial powerhouse of Spain. As Hugh Thomas has written, at the beginning of his history of the Spanish Civil War, "The 'Catalan question' would .... not have become acute once more had it not been for the development of Barcelona as the centre of Spanish industrialism. Irritation with the incompetence of the central Government at Madrid, as well as with the high tariffs demanded by Castilian landowners to protect their wheat and olives, led the new rich of Barcelona at the turn of the nineteenth and twentieth centuries to become Catalan nationalists. The Catalan language, customs and artistic traditions were feverishly revived. This, together with the Anarchist faith of the workers and the demagogic atmosphere inculcated by the Radicals made Barcelona at the turn of the century the wildest city in Europe."

In the early years of the new century, there was widespread rioting in the city, encouraged by the newly-formed Anarchist CNT party. This led, in due course to the dictatorship of Primo de Rivera, who immediately banned all political parties. Not un-naturally, this further enflamed the discontent in Catalunya, the most politically sensitive of all the Provinces of Spain.

This situation was exacerbated by the Great Depression and the subsequent slump. This hit Spain hard in 1929 and 1930. There was a decline in industrial production of over 30% and exports fell by two-thirds. This, in turn, caused the collapse of the government led by the dictator Primo de Rivera and his Finance Minister, Calvo Sotelo.

In turn this financial crisis hit the Carrau wine interests hard, for they had come to rely largely on export sales and they suffered seriously as a result. There was intense pressure on the banks as many investors, lacking any confidence, withdrew their deposits. In turn, the banks called in their debts; as a result Juan Carrau and his wife left everything and decided to create a new life for themselves in Uruguay.

It appears however that the main motivation behind the move to Uruguay came from Juan Carrau Sust's father-in-law, Juan Pujol. He and his wife travelled with their daughter and family and it was his personal contacts that were to find employment for the immigrant Carraus when they arrived in Montevideo.

Whilst this might have been the departure of the last of this branch of the Carrau family from Vilassar, the name is still present in the town and on St. Sebastian Street itself. There is the hairdressing business of Sr. Joaquim Carrau Garcia. He started this business having been an illustrator for comics. Interestingly enough his great-grandfather, born in 1865, was a painter and decorator in the town and the accounts of Francisco Carrau Mir in 1891 showed that he had given work to a certain Sr. Carrau *pintor*.

The Carrau diaspora in Spain is now centred on Valencia where Ignacio Carrau established an important law practice and where a member of the family is now a television presenter. There are also branches of the family in Calatayud, though it is no longer involved in wine production there, Mallorca and Barcelona. However our story now moves across the Atlantic once again to Montevideo.

CHAPTER II

Across the seas:
Montevideo.

View of the port of Montevideo in 1929.

Juan Carrau Sust.

Before we welcome Juan Carrau Sust and his family to the quayside at Montevideo, it might be of interest to look briefly at the history of wines in Uruguay up to that time and the conditions under which they were produced.

Of all the countries of South America, Uruguay was the one that attracted the least attention of the two great colonial powers on the continent, Spain and Portugal. The main reason for this was that it appeared to have little in the way of natural resources, particularly minerals. A further major disincentive may have been that the natives appeared to be particularly hostile: Juan Solís, the first Spaniard to try to establish a settlement there, was massacred, with all his followers, by the local Charrua Indians in 1516. In the following century there were developments on the fringes of the country as the Jesuits established a chain of mission-stations along the banks of the River Uruguay and, in a bid to limit the expansion of Spanish power, the Portuguese built a fort across the River Plate from Buenos Aires, in the town that is now called Colonia.

Whilst it is probable that the Jesuits, as elsewhere, planted vineyards to provide themselves with communion wine, there are no records of this having happened and the first written mention of wine production does not occur until 1776, more than two centuries after it is first produced in Mendoza and 170 years after vineyards were first planted just across the river in Buenos Aires. Independence did not come to the country until 1825, following a series of wars, first against Spain and then against Brazil.

Uruguayan produced wine was served at the inauguration banquet of the second President, Manuel Oribe, in 1835, but wine production did not really take off until the

1870's, when there was mass immigration from the strife-torn countries of Europe, particularly Spain and Italy. (The population of Uruguay more than doubled in the last quarter of the nineteenth century.)

At the same time, there was considerable investment in the infrastructure of the country, particularly by the British, who realising its pastoral potential, built the railways and the enormous slaughter-houses and meat-packing plants to support it.

It was, however, the immigrants from the Mediterranean countries who brought with them the traditions of wine-production and of wine-drinking. Many of them planted just rows of vines on their smallholdings to produce wine for their own family consumption. Wine was, without doubt, the preferred drink of the country. It has been estimated that the annual consumption was then about thirty litres per person; a figure that has been maintained until this day. (It should be pointed out that there was a powerful temperance movement in the country, during the first quarter of the 20th century. This led to a decline in the sales of all alcoholic drinks, which lasted for twenty years or more.) Whilst there were a considerable number of breweries in the country, it seems that the demand for their products came overwhelmingly from foreigners, particularly the British! One icon in the national drinks industry is Paso de los Toros tonic water. This was created, in the town of the same name, by, and for, the British engineers working on the railways.

Impulse was given to the wine industry, by the creation in 1871 of the *Asociación Rural del Uruguay (ARU)*. Alcides Beretta Curi has analysed the national origins of the committee members at the time of its formation and he gives them as four Uruguayans, two Frenchmen, two Italians, one German, one Catalan, two sons of Catalans, and one each sons of Italians, French and Spaniards. This international mix is representative of the diverse origins of the Uruguayan wine trade. This organisation is the ancestor of the *Centro de Bodegueros del Uruguay*, a grouping with which the Carrau family became closely linked.

Interestingly, amongst the members on the committee of this nascent organisation were four founding fathers of the industry: Francisco Vidiella, Pascal Harriague, Diego Pons and Pablo Varzi. Vidiella was born near Tarragona in Spain in 1820 and his family emigrated to Salto, in north-west Uruguay. At the age of thirty-seven, he moved to Montevideo and soon established a national lottery. Despite having no experience of producing wine, he then made an extended trip to Europe in 1873, bringing back with him an eclectic selection of vine-stocks, ranging from the Cabernet, Merlot and Garnacha to such rarities as the Fogoneus de Mallorca and the Quebranta-tinajas. With these he planted an experimental 36-hectare vineyard, alongside the newly-built railway-line, in Colón, a northern suburb of Montevideo.

Pascal Harriague.

His particular successes appear to have been with the Folle Noir and the Gamay Blanc, and, in his honour, the former variety is now known in Uruguay as the Vidiella. He celebrated the first National Vintage Festival at his winery in February 1883, but died the following year.

Harriague was born in Hasparren, in the Basses-Pyrénées *département* of France in 1819. He emigrated to Uruguay at the age of nineteen and two years later moved to Salto, where he established a tannery. This was destroyed in

1847 during the *Guerra Grande* civil war and he then earned his living by exporting precious stones. In 1874, he went to Concordia in Argentina, where successful, Bordeaux-style, wines were being produced. He brought back with him a grape called the Lorda, which was at the base of these wines and with which he planted a 200-hectare vineyard. This variety became widely adopted elsewhere in the country and its success was so great that it came to be known as the Harriague. In 1919 A.N. Galanti, in his book *La Industria*

Tannat

Vitivinícola Uruguaya recognised it as the Tannat, of Madiran in the French Pyrénées, and it has now become the 'signature' grape variety of Uruguay. Harriague's vineyard was all but destroyed by *phylloxera* and he retired to France where he died. His property passed on to two Englishmen, the Dickinson brothers, who replanted it and established there what was, probably, the first wine-laboratory in South America.

Diego Pons' father came from Minorca and his mother from Argentina. Whilst he was born in Montevideo, he spent five years of his childhood with his parents in Barcelona. At the age of eighteen, he qualified as an accountant and established a business exporting timber and fruit and importing *yerba mate*. He made powerful contacts in the twin worlds of masonry and politics, rising to being on the board of two banks, Minister for Rural Affairs, and finishing up as the country's Ambassador in Rome from 1925 to 1930. As far as his wine interests are concerned, he became President of the *Sociedad Vitícola Uruguaya* in 1891, just four years after it was founded to provide employment for those who had suffered from the recent enclosure of grazing land. (This under the name of Vinos de la Cruz was, until 2005, when it ceased producing wine, the winery with the longest continual history in Uruguay.) In addition, he became President of the ARU from 1894 to 1899.

Pablo Varzi was born in Montevideo in 1843, the son of immigrants from Genoa. At the age of twenty he set himself up in business making hats and, later, military uniforms. Given the history of the country at the time, this proved to be a particularly profitable line of business, enabling him to diversify and even to enter politics. In 1887 he, too, planted a vineyard in Colón. In due course he created the national Chamber of Industries, as well as the country's first wine co-operative cellar, the *Sociedad Cooperativa Regional de Viticultores*. Whilst this died, with him, in 1920, it does re-appear in our history. (Interestingly, the co-operative movement has never estab-

Pablo Varzi.

The Varzi Co-operative Cellars in Colón.

lished a firm foothold in the country's wine industry. It now accounts for less than 5% of Uruguay's production.) These four people show on what diverse roots the wine-industry of Uruguay was based!

In the years before the arrival of Juan Carrau in Uruguay, there had been a rapid expansion of the area under vines in the country. With the onset of *phylloxera*, there was a major shift in their location. The vineyards in the north of the country, particularly around the city of Salto, went into decline, whilst those around the capital, the *departmentos* of Montevideo and Canelones increased sharply, bringing them close to the urban market on which they relied.

The concentration of the vineyards around the capital was not because the soils, or the climate, were ideal for fine wines, but rather as a matter of convenience. As Daniel Bonfanti has written, "Although not all the regions in the country are suited to the production of grapes, we cannot justify this concentration either on climatic or geological grounds. With regard to this, the sandy soils, the high rainfall and the abrupt and severe changes in temperature, which are characteristic of the coastal zone, create a disadvantage for the cultivation of the vine, more especially because they help the spread of harmful diseases, such as *peronospora* (downy mildew), *anthracnosis* (black spot), etc.."

In a bid to minimise, the negative effect of, primarily, the climate, the Isabella, an American hybrid grape variety was introduced from Brazil in 1880, as well as some *labrusca* species. Because these thrive in a humid climate, they certainly make viticulture easier, but, sadly, they give large quantities of wine with a distinctive 'foxy' flavour. Even as late as 1989, the Isabella, known locally as the Frutilla, accounted for 20% of the production of Uruguayan wines, whilst an assortment of hybrids accounted for a further 25%.

What styles of wines were being produced in the country in 1930? Basically, these fell into two groups: firstly there were the 'light' wines which appeared on the market under a broad range of fanciful, mainly European titles, such as Champagne, Valdepeñas, Sauternes, Rhin and Borgoña. There were also the *vinos generosos* appearing as Jerez, Manzanilla, Oporto and *tipo* Sitges. These latter wines were generally 'manufactured' by being left outside in glass carboys to oxidise in the sun. One advantage was that this process helped mask the natural flavours of the wine. They were described as being produced in *soleras* and it is claimed that these were based originally on wines aged in vats, but which then underwent a form of fractional blending, with not more than half being drawn off at any one time, to provide continuity of style. This would seem to be a simplified system of that practised in the sherry region, with the main difference being the aging in glass, rather than oak butts. For Juan Carrau, who had himself made and sold *rancio* wines in Catalunya, this process would not

Solera wine production at Santa Rosa.

have come as a surprise. At that time very little wine was sold in bottle, most was sold in 5 litres *damajuanas*.

When the Carrau family arrived in Montevideo, it was logical that they should first turn to their relatives at Carrau y Cia.. Juan had no employment, but it seems that he was not seeking the life of a merchant prince with them, and he was able to offer to any potential employer the fact that he was certainly the only European-qualified oenologist in the country. However it was not his cousins who were to find work for him, but rather his father-in-law, who suggested that he might approach an old wine contact, the company Granja J.B.Passadore, in Colón. This company had been founded in 1898 by Bautista Passadore, who was originally a nurseryman.

Juan Carrau Sust was offered a position by this company as winemaker for his first vintage in Uruguay, that of 1930. He must have been successful in this role, for he was offered a full partnership and a ten per cent shareholding in the company the following year and it then adopted the rather ponderous title of Las Bodegas Hispano-Uruguayas launched the brand Santa Rosa de Passadore, Carrau y Mutio. It was not long before his shareholding was increased to 33%.

With his arrival, the company expanded rapidly. For the 1930 vintage, it processed just over 500 tonnes of grapes, by 1934, the figure had doubled and by 1938, it had reached 1,800 tonnes. The company also began exporting and it is interesting to note what he wrote in an article about an early shipment that they sent to Paraguay, "We should know that the types of wine sent to Asunción were Chianti and Rhine table wines, Oporto, Moscatel and Jerez fortified wines and Torino-style vermouth. It is symptomatic that repeat orders have only been received for the three

The first export order for Asunción, Paraguay.

A display of Santa Rosa and San Javier wines.

The Santa Rosa sparkling wine cellar.

Promotional material from the 1930's.

kinds of fortified wine: Oporto, Moscatel and Jerez. These are also the wines that we believe are best suited to being produced in Uruguay." Nevertheless, it was not long before the company was shipping 1350 cases of Cabernet to the United States on the s.s. Mormac Moon.

There were a number of factors that contributed to this rapid expansion of the company. Firstly, the improvement in the quality of the wines as the result of Juan's professional training must have made them stand out in the market. Secondly, and this must again be put down to his training at Vilafranca, in the heart of the *Cava* producing area of Spain, the company became the leaders in the rapidly growing sparkling-wine market.

The third reason, and this may well have come about because of the success of the first two, was that distribution of the wines was taken on by Carrau y Cía. Whilst they had been initial investors in the winery, they had been little more than sleeping partners. Now, with a diverse portfolio, that included not only such powerful spirits brands as Pedro Domecq and Martell brandies, White Horse Scotch Whisky and Gordon's Gin, but also Lipton's tea, Quaker Oats, Avanti Italian cigars and Dandicole & Gaudin tapioca, their sales-force had access to every outlet in the country. This new sales circuit must have had a dramatic impact on demand for their wines; a demand which sadly fell off after the distribution agreement was terminated in 1975, two years after the departure of Juan Carrau Sust's family.

Juan Carrau also firmly believed that added aging greatly increased the quality of the local wines; there had been a tendency for them to be released on the market too young. "As the annual production over the five year period 1928-1932 has been 19.74 litres per person and the consumption less than 19 litres, a stock has been created of

EL URUGUAY COLOCA VINOS EN ESTADOS UNIDOS

SE abren nuevos horizontes para la producción nacional, a medida que se va conociendo en el exterior la bondad de la misma. Y sumamente interesante es destacar el acontecimiento de que damos cuenta en estas líneas, puesto que se trata nada menos que de la colocación de vinos nacionales en los Estados Unidos de Norte América, rico mercado que ha empezado a valorar como corresponde la excelente calidad de los vinos que se producen en nuestro país, abriendo en esa forma una nueva ruta, próspera y vasta para los trabajadores del Uruguay.

Ha sido la importante firma de esta plaza, Passadore, Carrau y Muttio, bodegueros prestigiosos. los que han embarcado en la mañana de hoy, en el vapor "Mormacmoon" 1.350 cajones de vinos tipo Medoc, Rioja y Clarete viejo, con destino a Nueva York. Esta primera partida, será el comienzo de una etapa feliz, en donde los vinos del Uruguay podrán competir, dignamente, con los de los países americanos, con todo éxito. En la Exposición de Vinos de la Bolsa de Comercio, recientemente realizada, se vislumbró ya todo lo que podía hacer el Uruguay en la materia. Y es a los señores Passadore, Carrau y Muttio a quienes les ha correspondido el honor de realizar esta primera cruzada en beneficio de los viticultores ————

Wine leaves for the United States.

Catalina and her children — Quico, Mecha, José Luis and Malena Carrau, together with Rosa Saettone and her grandsons, Jorge and Toto Mutio.

12 million litres and this has undoubtedly been the main factor leading to better quality."

This rapid increase in sales demanded extra cellar-space and a vast construction project took place resulting in more than 20,000 square metres of cellars, filled with rows of vast vats of Nancy oak and an enormous yard with an army of glass carboys, full of wines gently oxidising in the sun.

The impression that Juan made on the industry was swift and deep. By 1932, he had produced the first bottle-fermented sparkling wine in the country, using native yeasts. In the following year, he published what he had learnt at wine-school in Spain in *El arte de la vinificación perfecta*, as a handbook for Uruguayan winemakers. In 1937, he arranged for Fr. Berreto, a priest and oenologist, to study in Mendoza. Following on these studies, he returned to Montevido, to establish a wine department at the Jackson Agricultural College. (Fr. Berreto's name is now honoured as that of the top range of wines from the company Bruzzone y Sciutto.) In addition in 1935, he took on the editorship of the bi-monthly trade magazine *Viticultores y Bodegueros*.

In articles he wrote in the revue, he offered advice on winemaking and his own personal political views. He foresaw a financial crisis in the industry; having lived through one in Spain, he was perhaps in a better position than anyone to recognise the signs. Apparently he first raised the matter in 1935 and in August of that year, the Association passed a resolution that steps should be taken to protect the interests of the members. Two years later he was to write, "Two years have passed in which these resolutions might have been put into effect; these two years have been lost to indifference. The problems of wine production have no immediate solutions, but they are becoming critical."

AÑO XIII - No. 151
OCTUBRE DE 1937

REVISTA de
la UNIÓN de
VITICULTORES
BODEGUEROS

The magazine edited by
Juan Carrau Sust.

REVISTA DE LA
Unión de Viticultores y Bodegueros
del Uruguay

Dirección: JUAN CARRAU SUST — Administración: SAETTONE y DIAZ

ABRIL - MAYO DE 1937

What he did suggest was that the state company ANCAP, which held a monopoly in the production of alcohol, might purchase increasing quantities of the surplus wine for distillation into brandy. Additionally, he proposed that the state might build regional co-operative wine cellars, which could take up the surplus wine and age it, thus making it more palatable, both for the domestic and export markets.

In the January 1939 edition of the *Revista,* it was announced that Sr. Carrau was having to relinquish his post as editor due to ill-health. He had worked himself into the ground. The following year he suffered a serious stroke and was severely paralysed. For the remaining twenty years of his life he was unable to move and was cared for by his wife and his oldest daughter Mercedes. (After his death, the latter retired to a convent and ultimately became the Superior of the Salesian Order of nuns in South America.)

This was a sad end to the career of someone who, in his forty three years, had wielded a great influence on two wine regions ten thousand kilometres apart. It was he who created the bridge for the Carrau family between Spain and Uruguay If in no other way, the name of Sust is honoured in the name of their top *méthode champenoise* sparkling wine.

Demonstration by wine-growers outside the home of President Terra, October 1937.

Juan Angel Mutio, Juan Carrau Sust and Albérico Passadore supervise the loading of a lorry.

Juan Carrau Pujol.

The incapacity of Juan Carrau Sust meant that his oldest son, Juan Carrau Pujol becoming nominal head of the family at the age of just sixteen. This meant that his formal education finished and he began working at Santa Rosa representing the third interest that his family had in the company.

What was now the company that he was joining? Amongst the family documents is a booklet that it prepared for the 2nd Industrial Exhibition, which took place in São Paolo, in August 1941. In this there is a detailed profile of the company. Annual sales totalled more than half a million *pesos*, with thousands of cases of still and sparkling wines being sent to North America, the cellars could stock three million litres, whilst, at the same time there were tens of thousands of carboys in the courtyard for the production of *vinos generosos*. For the sourcing of their wines, they owned 45 hectares of vineyards, but they accounted for no more than a tenth of their needs. All this was run by a workforce of 65 people. As a product additional to wine, they sold Mostina grape juice which, they claimed, "invigorates the young"!

What of the future? This, too, was made clear. "Mature wine from old vats will be our motto for the future." The workforce might rise to a hundred or more – though it should be pointed out that the company was already beginning to suffer from militant trade unionists. The brochure finishes with a statement of faith: "As in the great wine-producing countries, our wines are not just the product of a single vineyard, but from selected vineyards, after which no pains are spared in their treatment. From our long experience, this is the only route to take to guarantee each year the same 'style'." *Consistency* rules – O.K.!

Celebrations for the 50th anniversary of the founding of Santa Rosa, with a young Juan Carrau at the side of the priest.

There seems to have been quite a Santa Rosa cantonment alongside the main road in Colón. As well as the extensive cellars and production facilities, there were also the offices and three large family houses; once each, side by side, for the Passadores, the Carraus and the Mutios. A Uruguayan cousin remembers how impressed he was by the enormous crib that his Spanish cousins used to construct each Christmas.

In due course, these houses were to be flanked by two new companies created by Juan Carrau Pujol. Firstly there was a chicken hatchery, entitled Avícola Santa Rosa, and the current generation of Carraus can remember the excitement when the initial consignment of chicks arrived from Britain. This led, in the course of time to the establishment of a chicken co-operative CANAVI, of which he became President. Secondly, there was the creation, with his uncle

Francisco Carrau Sust, a chemist who had lived in Havana in Cuba since 1914, of Fanaproqui, a company making agricultural chemical products. This company is still in existence.

In November 1948, Juan Carrau at the age of 24, married Elena Bonomi , the 18 year old daughter of one of Montevideo's leading Italian families, the Bonomis. They were successful importers of spices, with offices not just in Montevideo, but also in Buenos Aires. (The family has played an important role in Italian history, for they were deeply involved in the fight for independence. The socialist politician Ivanoe Bonomi was a leading opponent of Mussolini and was hand-picked by Winston Churchill to lead the Italian government at the end of the Second World War. More recently, a branch of the family owned the factory producing Ducati motor-cycles.)

Juan Carrau Pujol and Elena Bonomi

Juan Carrau Pujol also was a racing pigeon enthusiast and it was always a priority for him to set the pigeons free from their loft twice a day. Racing pigeons was not a widely followed sport in the country, but he used to compete regularly, dispatching his birds to the furthest parts of the country, for eventual release to make their way back to their home loft called *El Rumbo* (The Route)

He was intensely proud of his multi-national origins. On one occasion, in a board-meeting, when someone referred to him as "El Gallego Carrau" (the Carrau from Galicia), he is said to have replied, "Galician I am not, I am an Uruguayan, born in Spain and, in any case, I would be a Catalan, never a Galician." One of the slogans of the company was: "Just at the same level as Italy and France, Spain and Portugal, Santa Rosa produces national wines."

It was not long before he was promoted to be managing director of the company, where he was affectionately known by all as Quico. His initial responsibility was to follow in his father's footsteps as winemaker. (Recently, there was an unexpected visit to the winery, by a former cellarman, now aged ninety-four, but still able to come on his bicycle. One of his memories is of having regularly to take samples to Quico "the chemist".)

By now, under the guidance of Juan, the oldest Mutio son, Angel, alias Toto, took on responsibility for the wine-making with Juan devoting most of his time to the his role as Managing Director, with particular responsibilities for the financial side of the business.

That he did not abandon totally his interest in the intricacies of wine production is make clear by the fascinating memories, written down in 2004, a then young oenologist the company had recruited, a Sr. Malde. Telling of the arrival of Toto he says of Quico, "Nevertheless, he did not give up totally his role in the technical side of the business, but reserved a certain niche for himself by maintaining contact with the suppliers of a number of important ingredients for wine production. This specialised knowledge was part of his inheritance from Vilassar de Mar…" It seems that the four fields of particular interest were sugar for the sparkling wine *dosage*, walnuts, wine-vinegar and communion wine!

For their sparkling wines, 'candy' sugar of the purest quality was needed. "For Santa Rosa, this candy sugar was produced by a small sweet manufacturer, Sr. Antonio Santalucci, and the dealings with him were always the exclusive preserve of Quico. Whilst he might delegate the physical part of the process to me, final control of the operation always remained in his hands. He gave me the responsibility for co-ordinating the ingredients and for grinding the sugar-crystals for mixing with the liquor."

As for the walnuts: "For making some of the fortified wines, as well as some of the ordinary ones, an infusion of walnuts was necessary. This was made from nuts that were provided by a dear, picturesque old Yugoslav, Juan Krusich, who grew them on his venerable old nut-trees in the town of Rosario. Every year, at the beginning of December, he would arrive at the Bodega and ask to speak to Juancito, as he called Quico. On one of these visits I was introduced to him, so that I could see to the final delivery of these precious nuts which he always said that he would send 'when the kings have passed' (that is, after the Twelfth Night), or in early January. After this I was made responsible for the dealings, but Juan Krusich wanted to have no discussions unless they were in the presence of Juancito."

Amongst the products that Carrau and Cía distributed was Savora 'French' mustard which was made under licence by an associated company Atlantis Ltda.. For this, they needed

Juan at a tasting at Santa Rosa cellar.

wine vinegar and they gave Santa Rosa a detailed specification of what they required. It seems that Juan was less than happy about entrusting the production of this to Toto and therefore assumed total responsibility for this business.

One of his cousins, described Juan as having "a firm religious base" and this was certainly true as he was one of the two signatories of the foundation document of the ACDE (Asociación Cristiana de Empresarios – The Christian's Businessmen's Association).

It was probably because of this that he insisted on Santa Rosa offering a range of Communion wines. These were never a big seller and at one meeting "Don Antonio commented that we had better things to worry about and that he had seen the Priest of Parque del Plata go into the sacristy with a bottle of Manchego Tinto, then the most common wine that the Bodega Santa Rosa produced."

Notwithstanding the negative attitude of his partners, he insisted that its production should be continued and overseeing this himself, even to the point that he dealt personally with the state monopoly ANCAP, about the grape-spirit that was used in its fortification, and coming down to the cellar to supervise the washing of the bottles.

His attention to detail must have been talked about in ecumenical circles, for he was soon asked to produce the country's first kosher wine…. under the close supervision of the local rabbi.

By this time the company had over 150 employees, rising to 300 at vintage time. Juan, was renowned for always being friendly and maintaining good relations with them and he is still fondly remembered for the Christmas parties that he used to organise for all the staff and their families.

It is clear the writer of this memoir worshipped Juan Carrau Pujol. "Take note", his mentor said to him, "that

Quico and Elena after a holiday in southern Brazil — a new project is conceived.

Toto is giving you plenty of scope to manoeuvre. Please, do not fail to take advantage of this." "I believe that I followed his advice and was soon taking on further responsibilities, using what he had taught me, just as if he were still my immediate superior."

Now, some sixty years later, one gets the impression that life during the latter days at Bodega Santa Rosa was not easy for Juan Carrau Pujol. There were conflicts of opinion with, and between, the Passadores and the Mutios, for Juan saw potential problems of succession, with all the three partners in the company having extensive families.

The Avícola San Martín de Porres was producing 10,000 chickens every two months for the ever-hungry *parrillas* of Montevideo. With the two oldest sons, Juan Luis and Javier, having to combine the university studies with being chicken-herds.

In addition to all these activities he was also a partner with Antonio Villamonte, Ferrúa and Reynaldo Delucca in Granja San Isidro Ltda, which owned two estates in Greater Colorado and Colorado, producing not just grapes, but also a broad variety of fruits and pigs. Further afield he was the first chairman of the Club Del Bosque in Punta del Este, as well as chairing the committee that promoted Maldonado *departmento*.

It is also apparent that he saw little future shackled to his current partners and that he had the ambition to focus solely on quality wines. The very fact that he had created companies in other fields, suggested that he had a restless mind and it must have come as a surprise to few people when, in 1971, at the age of 48, he resigned from the board of Santa Rosa, managing to sell his shares in the company whilst keeping for himself the initial investment that had been made in southern Brazil.

Politically, it was at this time that the left-wing guerrilla movement *Movimiento de Liberación Nacional,* more commonly-known as the *Tupamaros,* began to flex its muscles. In due course this led to a period of savage repression, led by the military, which in its turn caused the real value of wages to be halved and mass emigration of approximately a tenth of the population. It soon appeared that he had clear ideas for the future and, in the short term, it was not in Uruguay!

CHAPTER III

Across the Border:
Brazil.

In some ways Uruguay might be described as the Cinderella country of South America, for it is dominated by its two big neighbouring sisters, Brazil and Argentina, and its economy relies largely upon them. I am sure that the Uruguayans would not be unhappy with the metaphor, however, for they are happy with being small – and beautiful. As Tim Burford writes in the introduction to his guidebook of the country "Uruguay... has a permanent sense of being overshadowed by a larger, louder neighbour, while feeling deep inside that they are in fact the smarter, wittier, more creative ones. Indeed, the Uruguayan people are less party-loving than their neighbours in Argentina and Brazil, but more reliable and genuine, with a deep and innate sense of hospitality that delights all those who take the time to get to know them."

This sense of superiority implies no smugness, for any Uruguayan who is in any ways outward-looking accepts that it is to these neighbours that he should first look. In this way it is not at all surprising that Juan Carrau Pujol should turn to Brazil even before he decided to leave Santa Rosa. Compared to Uruguay, the size of the potential market for wine was limitless and there was little history of domestic fine wine production. There was one very good reason for this dearth of domestically produced fine wines, the climate.

In his book *Wine regions of the Southern Hemisphere*, written in 1985, Harm Jan de Blij, Professor of Geography at the University of Miami, described Brazil, as "Viticulture Emergent." However, despite the size of the country, almost equal to that of China, "There is no Mediterranean zone in the country, nor is there a dry climatic regime comparable to Argentina's Andean rainshadow." He continues, "Summers are moist and warm, winters are cool, and

"From their Italian birthplace to their new fatherland Brazil". – a mural painted by the Italian artist Aldo Locatelli, to celebrate the 1954 Grape Festival in Caxias do Sul.

there is no pronounced dry season to favour the ripening of grapes. Such a regime, propitious for the cultivation of many other crops, is not the best for viticulture. First the missionary settlers, then the Portuguese immigrants, and later the Italian winegrowers discovered this in turn."

As far as continuity in wine production in Brazil is concerned, it is this last group that is the most important. During the nineteenth century, there was a regular flow of refugees from the various states of Italy as the *Risorgimento* took place and revolution was widespread. Towards the end of the century, this flow turned into a torrent that was mainly directed to the southern Brazilian state of Río Grande do Sul. The fertile plains inland from the capital Porto Alegre had already been settled by German immigrants, so the Italians were forced to go further to seek land on which they could settle. For many this turned out to be

the hilly region of the *Serra Gaucha*, which reminded them of the natal Piemonte. Here, each family was granted a plot of land of twenty-five hectares and most of these were turned into general farms, with part being planted in vines.

Just as in many other wine-regions it was the arrival of the railway which gave impulse to wine production, with large companies, and, later, co-operative cellars, being established in the towns of Bento Gonçalves, Garibaldi, Caxias do Sul and Flores da Cunha.

When Juan Carrau Pujol first arrived in Brazil in 1967, he was aware of the climatic problems that the country posed as far as the production of fine wine was concerned and for the first six years he worked with the growers in the *Serra Gaucha*, to convince them of the merits of *vitis vinifera* grape varieties. He particularly pointed out the suitability of Merlot and Cabernet Franc as far as red wines were concerned. Here, he was working on his own for it was three years or more before the foreign multinationals perceived the merits of investment in the Brazilian wine industry. It was largely as a result of his pioneer work that this investment followed.

Whilst all the technical exploratory work that was needed might seem to be reason for the Carrau family not to invest in wine production in Brazil, the, on the face of it, unlimited potential for wine in the country, particularly with a rapidly increasing middle-class, with money to spend, must have appeared attractive. One other factor must also have helped. At that time the Brazilian government was protectionist and the import of wine was severely restricted. This limited the choice of what was available on the market.

There was a third very good reason for optimism; after the Carraus had split with Santa Rosa Uruguay, in 1972, they found their first joint-venture partner. For the leading multi-national wine and spirit companies of the world, there was one way of loosening the shackles that bound the import trade; that was by investing in the production of drinks within Brazil itself. Following Juan Carrau Pujol, the pages of the history of the wine-industry there are full of investment by such companies: National Distillers, Bacardi, Moet & Chandon, Heublein, Seagram, Pernod Ricard, and a host of others, have all had a major production presence in the state of Río Grande do Sul. For this project, the Carraus had as their minority partners the American giant, National Distillers, who took on a 20% participation.

This was a project on a grand scale; the company was entitled Vinhos Finos Santa Rosa S.A. and the winery was to be a vast castle complex complete with fortifications.

Quico and Elena with their eight children in1969 just after the Brazilian project came under way.

December 1968 – The site at San Siro, Caxias do Sul, is purchased.   March 1969 – Work begins on site clearance.

One source says that it was inspired by "the memorable French châteaux of the Middle Ages", whilst another has it modelled on an eleventh century Spanish castle. (Architecturally, it would appear to have rather more of the latter than the former.) Whichever of the two Château Lacave was, it came complete with a baronial hall and the most up to date winemaking equipment for making Brazil's first 'fine wine'.

The aim was to produce 50,000 cases of wine a year and the underground cellars had impressive rows of Nancy oak vats, which could hold 166,000 litres, in addition to this a number of oak barrels was purchased.

September 1969 – The ageing cellar begins to take shape.

Quico and Elena in Brazil – she was to play an important role as interpreter in the negotiations with National Distillers.

March 1969 – Note the stone blocks which are up to 1.2 metres wide and 2 metres thick.

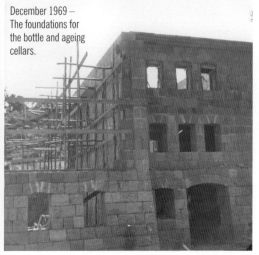

December 1969 – The foundations for the bottle and ageing cellars.

April del 72. Cirilo Calgary, the head stonemason, Lanrroso, the stone-merchant and Ricardo Ferrés a close friend of Juan.

September 1971 – Construction of the central part of the building begins, with its four towers, each 12 metres high.

January 1971 – Installation of oak vats with a total capacity of more than 100,000 litres.

December 1973 – Tasting and reception hall.

The official opening of the Château: Juan Carrau, with his aunt, Josefita Carrau, and his youngest daughter Margarita, unveils a plaque commemorating the eight generations of the family in wine production.

General view, 1974.

Construction began in 1968 and it was 1975 before it was officially opened and 1978 before it was completed. To start with, for the first two vintages in the 60's, the company rented cellars nearby for the production of the wines. The first wine to appear was a rosé, bearing the 1968 vintage, followed by some young whites of the same year. Their first top red wine was a 1971 vintage, which did not appear on the market until 1974.

The company did not own any vineyards but relied on approximately 150 growers for their grape supply. These were predominantly based in Caxias do Sul and Flores de Cunha, though white grapes were also sourced in Faroupilha and Bento Gonçalves.

One distinctive thing about the wines was their bottle. Some years previously, a cousin, Julio Carrau Ochoa, who was the representative for Grant's Scotch whisky in all Latin America, had returned from a visit to the Caribbean market with an empty Mateus bottle. This he showed to his friend Juan Carrau Pujol, who was impressed with it. As a result, the top wines of his new Brazilian venture came to be bottled in this *bocksbeutel*. These bottles did not, however, bear a label saying what they were. This information was given on a tag hanging from the neck of the bottle.

The product line was led by Château Lacave Velho do Museu. This was a red wine, a blend of 60% Cabernet Franc and 40% Merlot, never released before it was five years old, having spent eighteen months in vat, eighteen months in oak barrel and two years in bottle before appearing on the market. The first vintage of this to be released was the 1971. For more than twenty years, this was considered to be the country's outstanding red wine and there are still connoisseurs in São Paolo and Rio, who remember the wine and avidly seek out any bottles that might remain of these early vintages.

Below this was a range of four wines, entitled Ch. Lacave, two reds, a white and a rosé and two varietal wines called Anticuário: a Merlot and a Semillon. Lastly there was a medium-sweet *frizzante* white wine, Rhein Herr, a blend of Rhine Riesling, Welschriesling and Semillon. In later years they also produced wines franchised from Maxim's of Paris and had three of their wines listed by the French wine chain, Nicolas.

Not all these wines bore a vintage, as it is often claimed that there is a minimal difference between the vintages in Brazil and that many of the wines are blends of different years.

Nobres herdeiros de antiga estirpe.

Noble heirs of an old ancestry.

Château Lacave.
Para aqueles que só acreditavam em vinhos europeus.

Château Lacave. For those who only believed in European wines.

In Brazil there has always been seen to be a certain *cachet* attached to the drinking of European wines and the Lacave wines were specifically designed to appeal to this snobbery. "Château Lacave – For those who only believed in European wines" and "In Brazil, the first and only castle producing genuine château wine" were just two of their advertising lines. (This last slogan may well have been aimed at the Heublein product Castel Marjolet, which was enjoying great success at the time.)

In 1983, the French Cognac company Rémy Martin

A mediaeval pageant in the amphitheatre which is still used for Summer concerts.

purchased the 20% holding in Château Lacave from National Distillers and a further 30% from the Carraus making it a 50/50 joint venture. This relationship was to come to an end four years later.

As we shall see shortly, this was not to be the only

Ignacio and Juan Luis Carrau, the two brothers who worked at the Château supporting their father, together with Francois Hériard Debreuil.

Brazilian wine venture that the Carraus were involved in and Juan Carrau Pujol spent a hectic time between his home in Montevideo (the younger members of the family only came to Caxias at vintage time) and a series of sites in Brazil. At the same time he was developing the market for the wines and overseeing the construction of the 'castle'. It has been claimed by the Argentines that oenotourism in South America did not commence until 2000, but Château Lacave became a tourist attraction in its own right with 'farm-gate' sales providing useful additional income.

It is clear that the quality of the wine was recognised internationally, for the family archives contain letters congratulating the family from such notables as Louis Orizet, Professor Ribéreau-Gayon, José Domecq and Dr. Lamberto Paronetto.

The oldest son is Juan Luis Carrau Bonomi and it was

J'apporte un témoignage de haute satisfaction pour la qualité des vins de Château Lacave. Les yeux fermés, je les croirais Vins de France –

le 19 novembre 1975

Louis ORIZET
inspecteur général honoraire de l'Institut des vins de France, appellation contrôlée

I bear witness to my great happiness with the quality of the Château Lacave wines. If I had tasted them blind, I would have said that they are French.
Louis Orizet, Inspector General of INAO, France. 19th November, 1975.

En este ambiente medieval amenizado por vinos de calidad excelente es difícil expresar la gratitud que esta hospitalidad merece.

Mil gracias

22-X-78

In these mediaeval surroundings, designed for the production of excellent wines, it is difficult to express my gratitude for your hospitality. A thousand thanks. Marqués Don José Ignacio Domecq, Jerez de la Frontera, Spain
22nd October 1978.

Es muy emocionante ver, como el amor al vino ha logrado conjugar el arte y la tecnología dentro de este castillo, que en mi opinión representa el más hermoso homenaje al vino en America Latina.

17- mayo de 1981.–   Alejandro Hernández M

It is very moving to see how the love for wine has succeeded in marrying art and technology within this castle, which, for me represents the most beautiful homage to wine in South America.
Alejandro Hernández, Professor of Oenology, The Catholic University of Chile. March 1981.

Avec toute mes félicitations au Château Lacave pour les efforts réalisés et la qualité de ses productions.

En hommage amical de la vieille oenologie bordelaise à la jeune oenologie du Brésil qui fait la preuve d'un grand effort.

le 12 Janvier 1981

Prof. Pascal Ribéreau-Gayon
Directeur de l'Institut d'oenologie de
l'université de Bordeaux.

My congratulations to Château for what they have achieved and for the quality of what they are
producing. With the homage of the old oenology of Bordeaux to the young oenology of Brazil. Professor
Pascal Ribéreau Gayon, Director of the Faculty of Oenology,
Bordeaux University, France. June 1981.

Complimenti più vivi per il proprietario del Château Lacove e per i suoi vini ben vinificati e conservati. – In modo particolare il mio plauso per il Vinho Velho do Museu che ricorda le vecchie tradizioni europea la quale ha una buona partecipazione italiana (il nome dei Bonomi lo conferma!)

Con stima   _Lamberto Paronetto_
12 Luglio 1981   _(tecnico enologo Veronese)_

Congratulations on the wine to the owners of Château Lacave. The wines are well made and have
aged well. In particular I would like to applaud the Velho do Museu wine, which reminds me of the
of old European traditions so well represented here by the Italian name of Bonomi. With respect, Dr.
Lamberto Paronetto, Italy. August 1981.

he who was largely responsible on the spot for the operation of Ch. Lacave. When this was sold, he created a new wine business in Brazil, Vinícola Cave Velho Museu Ltda.. This has two vineyard holdings: one close to Caxias do Sul and the other, run organically, up near the Uruguayan border. From these he produces a Cabernet/Merlot blend, a Gewürztraminer and a Semillon. He manages his wine interests at the same time as being a professor of Biotechnology at Caxias University.

Juan Luis has seven younger brothers and sisters; coincidentally two of these, Ignacio and Gabriela, have followed him and now live in Brazil, a third, Inés lives in Spain and a fourth, Elena, farms cattle with her husband. This leaves three still involved in running the family wine business based in Montevideo: Javier, Francisco and Margarita. Javier trained as an agronomist and now manages the company. Francisco, studied microbiology and wrote his doctorate thesis on aromas. He now lectures on a regular basis at

A group including, Juan Carrau Pujol, Dr. Harold P. Olmo, Prof. Washington Babuglia and Juan Luis Carrau.

the university in Montevideo and oversees the winemaking. Youngest sister, Margarita, took her degree in communications and now spends much of her time promoting oenotourism on a national scale within Uruguay. There are currently five partners in the company: Javier, Gabriela, Ignacio, Francisco and Margarita.

Whilst Juan Luis, was looking after Ch. Lacave, his father involved Javier, from 1973 to 1975, in another big project in Brazil, with, once again, National Distillers as partners, this time represented by their vineyard subsidiary Almaden. Impetus was given to this project by the fact that the Brazilian government had recently doubled the duty on imported wines, in a bid to stimulate investment in the domestic industry.

Juan Carrau Pujol was entrusted with the task of seeking out the most suitable land in Brazil for a substantial vineyard. To help him he had Professor Olmo, a grapevine geneticist from the University of California, who had been a consultant to the wine industry in Uruguay for the past seventeen years and who had come, coincidentally, to southern Brazil during the Second World War, sent by the U.S. government to find potential land for agricultural expansion, should the American larder become bare.

The area they chose was near the cities of Bagé and Piratini. Bagé is a town of some 100, 000 inhabitants on the main road from Porto Alegre to Montevideo, lying, some 200 kilometres inland, 60 kilometres north of the border with Uruguay. In many ways this seemed to be ideal. Whilst the temperature was slightly higher than, for example, in the Serra Gaucha, it rarely exceeded 25C. or went below 5C.; thus there was little risk of frost damage, but winters were cool enough for the vines to profit from a period of dormancy. More importantly, whilst there was rain throughout the year, at its maximum it less than half that of the Serra Gaucha. The soil, ranging from sand to gravel, was free-draining and there was a minimal expectancy of either *phylloxera* or nematodes. As many as 20,000 hectares were considered suitable for planting, but the initial trial plot of vines was no more than 20 hectares. Shortly afterwards, however, this was tripled in size.

A Boeing 707 was chartered to bring in to Bagé a cargo of 70,000 virus-free, heat-treated and clonally-selected vines; a selection of all the classical varieties. These were flown to Porto Alegre and then shipped to Bagé in four refrigerated trucks. The intention was that the vineyard should be supported by a 14 hectare vine nursery, but, in the event, the trial was a flop and the whole vineyard was abandoned, with the project moving to Santana do Livramento and Cerro Chapeu.

Not deterred by this, and hoping to sell on the back of their wine products a broad range of their spirits within Brazil, in 1976, National Distillers purchased 1,200 hectares of grazing land at Palomas, some ten kilometres from the city of Santana do Livramento, 170 kilometres to the north-west of Bagé.

Santana is fascinating town. It used to claim the title of "the corned beef capital of the world" and it also has the distinction of having the oldest golf-course in Brazil, established by British managers in the canning plants. It lies right on the frontier with Uruguay and is joined, as a Siamese twin, to the Uruguayan city, and provincial capital, Rivera. As Paul Terhorst wrote for *International Living* in 2007, "We started in Rivera, which is just across the street from Livramento, Brazil. Literally. Most paired border towns have a river or a canyon… or something… between them, often with an immigration checkpoint. Think Laredo/Nuevo Laredo for example. But in Rivera/

The Boeing 707 arrives at Porto Alegre airport with its cargo of 70,000 vines.

The vines are examined under microscope.

Juan Carrau Pujol planting the first vines at La Mañana, Santana do Livramento, Cerro Chapeu.

Young vine plantations, Cerro Chapeu, Brazil.

Livramento, this side of the street is Uruguay; that side, Brazil. One side Spanish, the other Portuguese. One side takes *pesos*, the other *reales* and visitors and locals pass freely from one side to the other." Depending on how the local currencies are standing, you eat and sleep and do all your shopping on one side of the border or the other. The Uruguayan side has rows of duty-free shops and a smart new casino and hotel have just been opened to attract the high-rollers from Brazil! They look down on a sort of no man's land on the border where there is a not very savoury market, manned by Chinese from Paraguay, selling cheap products from their homeland.

The scale of National Distiller's project can be gathered by some of the figures. At its peak, 730 of the 1200 hectares were planted with 52 different grape varieties, but it was not until 1983, ten years after National Distillers first planted there that the first Brazilian Almaden wine appeared on the market. Of the 52 initial varieties, just eleven survived. Interestingly Professor Harm Jan de Blij, wrote in his book which appeared that same year, "In the 1980's the large scale venture of National Distillers, in the especially favourable microclimate of Santana do Livramento promised to produce 2.5 million gallons of quality wine for the domestic Brazilian market, representing fully one fifth of current local consumption."

Unfortunately, everybody's optimism seems to have been misplaced. As happens so frequently when a wine company is owned by a distiller, illogical decisions appear to have been made and National Distillers, who had so far invested $60 million in the project, sold Almaden Brazil to Canadian distillers, Seagram, for $14 million. The owner of that group, in due turn, decided he would rather be a media mogul and sold to French distiller, Pernod-Ricard. Now the vineyards belong to the Brazilian Miolo company which is based outside Bento Gonçalves, but also has interests in vineyards in the subtropical São Francisco valley. They have been backed in this venture by a major industrialist, Randon, from Caixas do Sul.

Despite this powerful retreat by a series of multi-nationals, this region still hosts five wineries on the Brazilian side of the border, as well as four on the Uruguayan. Access to them is now much easier for whilst Bagé airport may have no scheduled flights, Rivera International Airport, on the Uruguayan side of the border now has regular connections to Porto Alegre, Montevideo and the world!

Now, more than thirty years after Juan Carrau Pujol's vision for the region, and National Distiller's major investment there, Campanha, as a whole, is considered by many as the future for the fine wine industry in Brazil. Adriano Miolo, has described this as "the new

California." A total of sixteen wineries are based there and they account for 15% of the fine wine production of the country.

Whilst the Carrau family might have initially suffered a couple of setbacks in Brazil - they have come back there – as we shall see.

CHAPTER IV

... and home again.

Montevideo

The new Juan Carrau premises in Colón.

In its edition of Saturday 12th May 1976, Uruguay's leading newspaper, *El País*, carried a photograph and an article which began, "Last Wednesday there was the official opening at Cesar Mayo Gutierrez 2556 of the modern Bodega Juan Carrau, by the Minister of Industry and Energy, Ing. Quim. Luis H. Meyer."

Whilst Juan Carrau Pujol may have left Santa Rosa in 1971 and had recently concentrated his efforts into the two projects in Brazil, it had never been his intention to abandon winemaking in Uruguay. Indeed, the family still owned more than 20 hectares of vineyards on fertile black soils, at Las Violetas, some 40 kilometres or so to the north of Montevideo along Ruta 5.

The previous year, he had purchased the winery that Pablo Varzi had built for himself 120 years before, but which, since his death, had been largely abandoned, most latterly serving as a tobacco drying warehouse. Coincidentally it lay less than a kilometre away from the Santa Rosa cellars, further along the

The official opening of the new bodega, Juan Carrau and Ing. Quim. Luis H. Meyer, Minister of Industry and Energy.

same main road, away from the city centre, but on the other side.

The title of this new company was Vinos Finos Juan Carrau S.A. and right from the outset, the objective of the winery was to produce nothing but *vinos finos*; by this was meant just wine made from *vinifera* grapes and only in bottles, rather than the ubiquitous five-litre demijohns that then, and still largely now, dominate the Uruguayan domestic market.

Any wine that they might produce of lesser quality would be sold in bulk to other merchants.

In the early days they relied on classic European names for their range of products, which included Chianti Luigi Bonomi, (named in honour of his father-in-law) Cava de Varzi Chablis and Rioja and ... Dubonnet. It would appear that the company was the agent for this product in Uruguay and that a decision was taken that it should be produced locally, under licence, in a bid to increase sales on the South American market. Vinos Finos Juan Carrau were entrusted with its production. An initial shipment was made of 500 cases of the Uruguayan-produced wine to Buenos Aires, but then a group of Mendoza wine producers lobbied against any further shipments to Pernod Ricard in Argentina, despite agreements that permitted such trade. There was a similar situation with regard to Brazil, which also refused to accept a shipment. Unfortunately ambition had been overtaken by politics and, as a result, the Uruguayan export statistics for the year 1979 show a most surprising

The initial product range.

Women on the bottling line for the first export order.

Juan Carrau and his son
Javier by their first shipment
for export.

Dubonnet leaves for Nigeria, 1979.

blip, when they record the export of 20,000 cases of wine to Pernod Ricard in Nigeria. It appears that this country was then one of the leading consumers of Dubonnet!

It was not long, however, before the company abandoned European names for its wines and began to proudly promote their own brands as being distinctively Uruguayan, with the Tannat grape as the main weapon in their armoury. Early after his arrival in the country Juan Carrau Sust had recognised the potential of this variety, when, writing in an article in 1937 about wine best suited for the local market, had said, "With regards to this, we can say that the best adapted grape is the Harriague, or Tannat, with which, without changing the grape-variety, but rather the ways of treating it, has demonstrated that it can produce unsurpassable wines, appealing to the consumer and without a hint of harshness..."

At about the time of the creation of Vinos Finos Juan Carrau, the Uruguayan government commissioned Professor Denis Boubals of Montpellier University to conduct a study of the country's vineyards. His conclusion was "If you don't change your plants and the management systems for your vines, this viticulture will die within a few years." The Carraus had already appreciated this and were the leaders in improvements not only in the vineyards, but also in the cellars and laboratories.

One immediate way in which they were able to improve the quality of their Tannats was by barrel ageing.

The first Tannat del Museo, 1979.

It was this company that was the first to produce *reserva* wines by investing in small oak barrels rather than relying on historical enormous oak vats. Their first barrel-aged Tannat del Museo appeared in 1979, under the brand name Castel Pujol.

As has already been mentioned the soils and the climate of the vineyards close to Montevideo are ideal for the production of fine wines, if it is strictly controlled. As Monty Waldin says, "The generally clay-rich soils and warm climate combine to give wines with markedly high levels of alcohol, and crisp, direct fruit characters." These vineyards can be compared to those of Bordeaux in many ways, but the major difference is the richness of the soil. Without careful vineyard management, the yields can be excessive, with a resultant drop in quality of the wine. As far as sales on the domestic market at that time were concerned, this was of little importance. At the time over half the Uruguayan wine consumed in the country was *rosé* or *clarete* – somewhere between rosé and red. Often the base grapes for these wines were lesser varieties such as Muscat d'Hambourg. Now tastes have changed some-what with a distinct move towards, at the quality end of the market, red wines.

In many ways, Uruguay is no different from other wine-producing countries, as far as consumption of the product is concerned: there is the everyday wine drunk as a matter of course by the majority of people, and there is the 'better' wine drunk by the wealthier classes. I put better in inverted commas, because this may just be the percep-tion of the consumer. As has already been seen with regard to wine consumption in Brazil, fashion dictated that those who could afford to, drank imported wines.

Juan Carrau, with his youngest son, Francisco, who began working in the company laboratory the year before he went to university.

CHAPTER V

Up Ruta 5

Rivera

Juan Carrau Pujol.

In 1922, the French wine industry was going through one of its periods of crisis and a 'Week of Wine' was held in Paris to consider how it could regain lost markets. Even the Uruguayan market was considered: "In all Latin America, the ordinary man in the street is not a customer for French wine... The labourer, the worker in town and country in Argentina, Uruguay and Chile likes drinking a rough, red wine, which is produced locally and which gives him satisfaction. As opposed to this, in the higher classes of society, wherever our moral influence is felt, our wines are sought out and considered to be the essential accompaniment to all celebrations, banquets and meetings. The taste that the upper classes in Latin America have for our wines bears witness to their delight in French culture..." Whilst both arrogance and ignorance appear in equal measure in this statement, there is a core of truth: many consumers believe that imported wine is good, domestic wine is less good.

Fifty years later, Juan Carrau Pujol not only wanted to overcome this prejudice within Uruguay, but he also sought to produce wines that would hold their own in international markets. To achieve this he wanted to find the best location

Professor Larry Bolger of UC Davis and Javier Carrau with vinestock recently arrived from the U.S.A. and France.

within the country for the production of wines that could realise this ambition, but he also was determined to select the best source material for them and to insist on the most up to date techniques in vineyard and cellar.

In a bid to find the ideal vineyard site, he dispatched his second son Javier up to the Brazilian frontier, some 500kms. north of Montevideo, to search it out – he did have the advantage of having spent some time there with Professor Olmo on the far side of the border. The brief was to find 50 suitable hectares of land that could be planted with vines. At the end of nine months, he reported back, having located, with the help of the agronomist Professor Babuglia, an ideal site of 307 hectares, some ten kilometres east of the provincial capital Rivera, beyond the airport. This land was bought in 1975 at a price of $US300 per hectare, and the parcel of land was rounded off by the purchase of a further 35 hectares, but this time at the inflated price of $US400 per hectare. This property has been named Cerro Chapeu, which is Brazilian for 'bowler hat'. Why bowler hat? - because of the distinctive shape of a number of hills in the region, where the sandstone has been eroded over millennia.

What, apart from the price, was appealing about this land? Firstly, the soils were poor, but free-draining sandstone. This enabled the roots to go deep into the earth to find moisture, even in the driest seasons. Also, this would mean lower yields of better-quality grapes. Secondly, the altitude of the vineyards, at just over 300 metres above sea-level, meant that there were not only greater temperature differences between the seasons, enabling the vines to gain winter rest, but also between day and night, leading to increased fruit flavours in the grapes. Spring frosts in September are not unknown. Interestingly enough, in 1937 Rivera was

A 'bowler-hat' hill of Cerro Chapeu.

A boundary marker between Uruguay and Brazil.

Morning mists over the highest vineyards in the country.

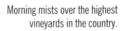

Heavy frost in July.

one of only two *departmentos* in the country where there were no vineyards. This was still the case when the Carraus arrived more than thirty years later.

To reach the winery, you must travel some distance along a dirt road. Here the boundary between Brazil and Uruguay is marked by the watershed and a series of concrete markers. The road winds between these and you cross the border on a number of occasions – fortunately there are no controls or formalities! The drive leading off to the vineyards lies between boundary markers 610 and 611. Whilst, at the time, there were no other wineries in the region, now three others have sprung up, two of them on the far side of Rivera and one on the way to Cerro Chapeu.

The importance of this development in Uruguayan viticulture was recognised by the government in a Decree, dated November 19th 1977, as being a 'Plan of National Interest'. On a site of 306 hectares, 100 hectares of vines were to be planted as a 'model in the country'. These vines were to reach maximum production by year eight.

On the estate, there was already a small farmhouse and Javier established himself there to oversee the planting of the vines. After some twenty years a guest-house and a winery were built. The latter was constructed to absorb the production of fifty hectares and this has now been achieved.

The fact that there was a substantial amount of land available for planting meant that the ideal site could be selected for each variety. As Francisco Carrau says, "We planted the parcels on very specific spots on the hillsides to get the best sun and ventilation for each variety. There can be up to a month's difference in picking times due to different slopes." One potential problem envisaged was the predominant south wind, so windbreaks of pine and poplar were planted where necessary.

For the planting, selected clones of virus-free plants were imported from nurseries in California, France and South Africa. The predominant varieties were Chardonnay and Sauvignon Blanc for white wines, and Cabernet Sauvignon, Merlot, Pinot Noir and Tannat for red wines. However there are also plantings of such lesser varieties as the Muscat Miel (or Muscat Giallo) and the Arinarnoa, a cross between the Merlot and Petit Verdot grapes. As far as the national grape, the Tannat, is concerned nine different clones have been imported from France. In addition there have been planted four historic Urguayan clones recovered by Francisco Carrau from 130 year-old vines originally planted by Harriague. These are micro-vinified, in order to study the individual characteristics that they give to the ultimate blended wine. The importance of this particular research was declared of national interest by the Uruguayan Ministry of Education and Culture, in 2006.

In a bid to extract the maximum potential from the grapes, each year two green harvests are carried out. Experiments are also carried out with pruning techniques, most vines being planted along low wires. Some Muscats, however, are grown on the *parral*, or pergola, system. Elsewhere in Uruguay, many growers train their vines on the lyre system in order to minimise the effects of excessive humidity. Javier Carrau, however, is not convinced of the merits of this. Experiments are also carried out into replacing dead vines by layering, or *provignage*.

Initially, the grapes had to be trucked overnight to the winery in Colón for processing, but the Carrau brothers determined to build the most up to date winery in South America. The basic principal of this was to avoid the use of pumps. The whole process was to rely on gravity. In order to achieve this, they built the winery into the hillside, so that

May 1997 Excavations begin.

Francisco Carrau, Joao Luiz Rossignolo, project manager, Renzo Ciceri, Javier Carrau and Daniel Basile.

June 1997 The octagonal foundations take shape...

August 1997 ... and now the first floor...

September 1997 The earth is replaced around the foundations.

November 1997 ...with the stainless steel tanks and emerging central tower.

January 1998 The roof appears...

...and is completed.

The cellar ceiling.

The circular cellar, with its twin walls of brick.

cember 1997
e wooden
cking with
e tanks for
ception of the
rvest.

View of the completed winery with its four floors.

the grapes could come in at ground level at the top, either to be pressed, or to fall directly into stainless steel tanks at the second level, from which they could , if necessary, be drawn off into casks for maturation at the lowest level, dug deep into the hillside and lined with sandstone rock.

The winery, which was not completed until 1998, has been designed to fuse into the landscape, with a roof of soft green tiles and stone walls. It is octagonal in shape and all the processes can be supervised from an office/laboratory at the centre of the reception level. For red wine, increased colour and flavour is obtained by automatic *pigeage*, or pressing down of the cap of pomace.

In all there are 20 temperature-controlled, stainless steel tanks, though some are divided in two to facilitate the vinification of smaller lots of wine. On the lowest level there

The interior of the winery with the laboratory at the centre.

250 oak barrels for the maturation mainly of Tannat wines; half of these are French oak and half American. Currently they are largely of the traditional 225 litre size, though there are also some of 300 litres.

On the crest of another hill, the guest-house has been built around a rectangular courtyard, complete with swimming-pool and barbecue for the traditional Uruguayan *asado*. There are magnificent views to the south, over the vines and woods to the distant horizon.

The estate however is much more than just vineyards, a winery and a guest-house. They are just

Sunset at vintage time.

a part of a wonderful green whole. As Samantha Stokes described it in an article in Wine Magazine in 2007, "It seems as though everything has been thought of," – even to the extent that you can pay a virtual visit on their website!

There is a herd of 200 bullocks being fattened up for market – the Uruguayan beef is so good because the cattle spend their whole life grazing outdoors, meaning that they are generally slaughtered at three years old, rather than two. There is also a flock of 120 Romney Marsh and Hampshire Down (Caramora) sheep, some of them destined for consumption on the spot, and 26 quarter and criolla horses, though it appears that their numbers vary due to the predations of rustlers from across the border.

The guest-house reflected in the lake.

There is also a plantation of olive trees, though, currently, they appear unwilling to yield up a harvest, and, in the summer, a local apiarist sites up to 40 hives on the estate. The resultant honey is wonderful!

Another feature is the wildlife. A professional ornithologist spent a day and a half checking on the bird population: just in that short time he counted 160 different species and he believes there are many more.

The flock of Hampshire Down sheep.

Hereford steers by the vineyards.

Around the world there is no shortage of wonderful wineries. This one, nevertheless, must be amongst the most beautiful and also amongst those that are closest to nature. Its remoteness has meant that it is off the general Uruguayan oenotourism trail, but the recently established air route from Montevideo to Porto Alegre via Rivera means that it is now more accessible – and also that the silence of the site is briefly disturbed by the arrival and departure of the planes from the nearby Rivera Airport. The winery might also provide an attraction away from the tables for the visitors to the newly-opened casino in the town!

Historically, the company has sourced most of its grapes from its own vineyards, but, at the same time, has relied on a number of small growers in the Las Violetas region for further supplies. Now, having extended their own vineyard holdings there, and with Cerro Chapeu's vines coming to maturity, they only have a minimum number of growers, under the supervision of the Carrau viticulturalist, that they use for specialised individual varieties. For the future, there is still suitable land available for planting in Cerro Chapeu, and they anticipate that they will be all but self-sufficient in this direction for the foreseeable future.

A wintertime ride through the vines.

CHAPTER VI

... and back home again

"Your wines are even more impressive than before. Is clear that you are leading the way in Uruguay and I am enthusiastic about your progress in international markets."

Paul Hobbs, Healdsburg, California. March 10th 1995.

"Les Carrau ont fini de porter le Tannat au pinacle. Vine Castel Pujol-Vine Chateau Montus"

Alain Brumont, Madiran. December 25th 1998.

Castel Pujol was the first Uruguayan wine I ever tasted and I still have touch memories of its vibrancy and intensity. Your vines and your wines are an inspiration of the art of your industry.

Tim Atkin. February 23th 1999.

I little realized in 1993 when I tasted that "burly" 1988 Castel Pujol Tannat that you were forming the first small flames of a wine revolution. But you were. The revolution is now in full flow. It has a long way to go, but I am delighted to see you still leading the way.

Oz Clarke. Feb. 3rd 2002.

Friendship and family are the two most important things. Thank you for showing your wonderful family and wines to me. I will be sure to come back.

Linda Bisson, Prof. UC Davis, California. June 12th 2004.

"The Carraus were the first to realise that Tannat, a real delicacy, is Uruguay 's trump card in international markets".

Andre Domine 2012, Wines of Uruguay.

As we have seen Juan Carrau Pujol was intent on improving the image of his wines by paying more attention to their production. At the same time, he was helped by the results of a survey carried out in 1975 at the behest of the Organización de Vinicultores. The ultimate objective of this was to launch a publicity campaign to promote the drinking of wine. Diana Czapski, a specialist in 'Motivational Research', carried out this survey with eight focus groups of men aged 25 to 30 and 40 to 50 and housewives aged 20 to 30 and 40 to 50. The groups included both regular and occasional drinkers of wine.

Her report came up with four suggestions, not all of which were relevant to the objectives of Bodegas Carrau:

· Reduce the lack of confidence in basic table wines, by lessening their anonymity, by giving more information about their source, how they are produced, etc..

· Create different categories of wine which can be clearly recognised by the presentation.

· Take active steps to get women more interested in wine, pointing out the types of wine that, by their characteristics, might appeal more to them.

· Modernise the image of wine without destroying what it already had that was worthwhile.

Perhaps it is as well to continue with what efforts were being made to upgrade the image of wine at a national level, rather than that of an individual wine company. Just one year before the report came out, the first CREA came into being in the country. This concept was based on what was already happening in France and Argentina. It will consist of a small group of growers and merchants, working with an agronomist to improve techniques in the vineyard. This will mean regular visits to each other's vineyards, as well as studying the latest developments both at home and overseas.

From the outset, the Carraus have been very supportive of this idea and are members of the Grupo CREA Ing. Luis Fernández, which also includes a number of leading producers and is led by a technical assessor. Of the three CREAs currently in existence this probably is the most powerful.

Up to the year 1988 responsibility for wine lay with the Ministry for Livestock, Agriculture and Fisheries, but in June of that year INAVI (El Instituto Nacional de Vitivinicultura) was born. This had partly come about as an effort to strengthen the country's wine industry prior to Uruguay's accession to Mercosur – the South American Free Trade Zone. This, in turn, would let loose on the market the wines of Argentina, Brazil and, potentially, Chile, where vineyards were on a larger scale, yields were generally higher and the costs of production lower.

The brief of INAVI was three-pronged: to improve the quality of Uruguay's wine, to consolidate their consumption on the domestic, and to seek out export markets. Javier Carrau was the first representative on the body of the association of producers, Centro de Bodegueros del Uruguay, which had been founded as long ago as 1932 and which currently represents 16 companies in the Uruguayan wine trade. Between them, they own 17% of the vineyard land

and control 22% of the production and 90% of the export of wine.

All these formed part of the original objectives of Juan Carrau Pujol, when he established his new wineries, but, sadly he did not live to see this new programme; he had died in 1984 at the age of 60 after suffering, stoically, great pain for many months. As someone, in what might be considered to be a loose translation, said of him, "Juan Francisco was one of those people who leave an indelible vapour-trail in the sky after they have gone." It was he who had picked up the pieces, at a very young age, after his father's illness and who had seen that his own sons were in a position to create their own careers. It was he who laid the foundations for the company, and began to build on them.

What steps were taken to improve the image of Uruguayan wines at home and around the world? The first required little effort but meant much: Uruguay, in 1993, became the first country in South America to ban the use of foreign wine names, such as Chablis and Rioja, on their labels. Secondly, subsidies were given for the grubbing up of hybrid and American vines and their replacement with *vitis vinifera*. Thirdly, and this might well be as a result of the Czapski survey, wines were divided into two distinct classes. Higher-class wines, made from quality vinifera grapes, in 75cl. bottles (or less) and with a minimum degree of 11.5°, could be labelled as VCP, or Vino de Calidad Preferente. All wines, no matter from what grape they are produced, in litre bottles, tetrapacks or demijohns are described as Vino de Mesa. One result of the change in the nature of the vineyards is an improvement in the quality of the basic wines, Now many Vino de Mesa wines are made from noble grape varieties, whilst before they would generally be made from American or hybrid grapes.

With regard to consolidation on the home market, an advertising campaign was launched, literally at all levels. I have in front of me a car sticker, little larger than a visiting card, which bears three distinct messages, each with its own appeal: *El Vino Es Mejor* - Wine is Better; the nationalistic *Uruguayo y Natural* – Uruguayan and Natural. (This ties in with the general image of the country Uruguay – país natural: Uruguay, country of nature.) and *Bueno para el corazón* – Good for the heart. (We will look at the medicinal benefits of the country's wines later.) In addition on the radio and on posters, on public transport and by the roadside the message came over clear, *Tomate tiempo. El Vino: nuestro y natural* – Take time. Wine: Ours and Natural.

UruguayNatural

As for selling on international markets, the initial approach was to appear at international Trade Fairs. The wines made their international stage debut in 1989 at Anuga, an enormous food and drinks fair in Cologne. This debut was comparatively muted for they were allocated space on the Uruguayan national stand and were in competition with the better known beef and citrus products. However five companies, including Carrau, were there to show their products. This was followed up with a British première at the London International Wine Fair, where they had a small stand in a remote corner of the balcony. Uruguayan wines had arrived, but you had to look hard to find them!

It was felt that the unique selling point for Uruguay's wines was the Tannat grape – thus endorsing what Juan Carrau Sust had said more than 50 years earlier. Among the slogans they used for their international campaigns were *"El País del Tannat* – URUGUAY". "The land of Tannat – URUGUAY" and "The Tannat Country – Discover

Javier and Francisco Carrau
on the guest-house balcony.

Uruguayan flavour in its most typical wine of all: Tannat."

Javier was the member of the family to pack his suitcase and bring his passport up to date, to sell the wines around the world and, within the course of the next two or three years, he had introduced fine wines under the Carrau label onto such diverse markets as Sweden, Poland, China, Switzerland, Holland and the United States. Each market has demanded a different approach: for example in Poland large quantities of wine are sold through a wine club.

In Britain, it took longer for the first order to arrive, partly because of the weakness of sterling at the time. In 1993, however, a consignment of Tannat 1988 from Las Violetas was ordered by a major supermarket chain. This was the first Uruguayan wine to be sold in Britain and it met with favourable comment in the press from such leading critics as Tim Atkin, Oz Clarke and Hugh Johnson.

Some of the world critics comments are
the best recognition for Carrau

Sainsbury's has been trying to get something fresh and supple out of Uruguay. But neither country, with the splendid exception of Castel Pujol Tannat, has produced anything to worry Argentina, let alone Chile. Things like Castel Pujol Tannat 91 should be saved for a big lump of protein. Deeply coloured, meaty red with flavours of tobacco, chocolate and oak on the palate. Drinking beautifully at the moment. 5.15 Pounds.

Tim Atkin,
The Observer Magazine,
London, April 1995

Uruguay is an important producer for a population that loves wine as much as the Argentineans. It has a long tradition in vineyards, mainly with French varieties, including the Tannat of Madiran. The first quality producer is in the north of the country, Juan Carrau's vineyards are in Rivera, close to the border with Brazil. The Carrau Castel Pujol (Cabernet, Merlot, Sauvignon, Tannat, etc.) is sometimes found in the international market.

Hugh Johnson,
The World Atlas of Wine,
Fourth Edition, England 1995

I tasted the Castel Pujol, 88´ Tannat. This is the grape that makes Madiran, one of France´s most unapproachable reds. Yet the Uruguayan example was excellent, a purple red with dark burly plum fruit, some tannin, sure, but spice and richness too.

Oz Clarke,
Daily Telegraph,
Londres, June 1993.

This success in Britain had sad consequences on that market which are still being felt. This original Tannat had established a price for Uruguayan wines which was acceptable for the quality of the wine but well above the average price of ordinary wine on the market. (New Zealand had already established a healthy precedent, with no-one expecting to spend much below £10 for a bottle of wine from that country.) However other supermarkets approached Uruguayan producers and promised substantial orders if they could provide wines under the supermarkets' own labels at basic prices. This is a level at which, because of production costs, Uruguay is, at best, ill-equipped to compete. Wines were found, but at the expense of quality – both of the wine and of the packaging.

There was also a certain naivety, or perhaps worse, contempt for the consumers on the part of the purchasers. Perhaps it was an attempt to pass the wine off as Chilean that led one supermarket chain to call their wine Pacific Heights – a wine coming from the flattest country in South America and which is on the Atlantic seaboard.

The sad result was that for many of those British consumers who were adventurous enough to buy Uruguayan, their first taste was of a poor wine. This has not been forgotten and it something that Uruguay is still having to fight against. The markets of the world are awash with wine; why choose a wine from Uruguay?

Currently the company sells approximately 60% of its production on the domestic market and 40% abroad. In Uruguay itself, they have their own sales force operating in the two 'home' departmentos of Montevideo and Rivera, whilst in the other 17 they rely on regional distributors. The third brother, Ignacio, used to be responsible for the domestic market, but he now lives in Brazil and a General

Ignacio, Francisco and Javier – the three brothers on the Board of Directors, with their separate responsibilities, sales, production and exports.

Manager has been appointed in charge of this role.

For exports, the leading market is Brazil, where they have two different importers, each handling different product lines. There is a sales manager responsible just for this market. Elsewhere, Francisco concentrates mainly on the United States, whilst Javier indefatigably travels the rest of the world.

One important aspect the Carraus' importance in the South American wine industry that has been touched upon here and there, but not dealt with in detail, is their role as innovators and this is a role that is spread over many fields. One of the reasons for this may well be that, until the arrival of Juan Carrau Sust, wine production was based very much on the peasant traditions of their forefathers. He brought with him not only what he had learnt in the family vineyards, but also from his course at wine school in Vilafranca del Penedés, under his teacher Cristobal Mestre. His expertise had its earliest results in the production by

Santa Rosa of the first bottle-fermented sparkling wines in Uruguay.

In Brazil, Juan Carrau Pujol and his sons Juan Luis and Javier, led the field by liaising with Professor Olmo to seek out the best land for planting and by importing virus-free and clonally selected vines. In 1978 they established the first laboratory in the country to select the best yeasts.

In Uruguay, an early entry into world of green wine-making, was their use of the spent marcs from the presses as a composting fertilizer. In 1989 the family created the company Biofer to process this.

It is perhaps through Juan's seventh child, and fourth son, Francisco that we see this tradition of research and experimentation best expressed. He studied microbiology and wine biochemistry firstly at the Biological Sciences University of the Republic in Montevideo and later in Madrid. The thesis for his wine doctorate was on the microbiology of aromas not just relating to wine but also to food products.

Paul Henschke director of the PhD thesis in Aroma and Wine Microbiology made by Francisco Carrau. Photo at the Henschke family winery in Barossa Valley, Australia in 1999.

The company created its first research and development laboratory in Uruguay in 1985. In 2006 it received government support for the construction of the most advanced tasting room in the country in the form of 'laboratory of sensory analysis', to be followed the following year by a new laboratory at the home winery in Colón. containing the most up-to-date technical equipment.

What has all their research achieved? In the vineyards, they have worked with such international experts as Paul Henschke and Patrick Iland from Australia on questions of plantation management. They have recovered the DNA of the original Tannat vines that Harriague planted in 1870 and have developed clonal material from them. This work has been in conjunction with Semillas Santa Rosa S.A.. (Similar work has also been done with historic plantings of varieties such as Sousao, Teroldego, Muscat Miel and Nebbiolo – all plants that were brought over by the early immigrants to the country.) In the study of early Italian varietals they have been working with Beppe Versini at the Institute San Michele all'Adige and for Spanish with Bodegas Roda in Rioja.

More recently there has been work on the application of biological control of fungi in the vineyards with antagonistic yeast strains; the detection of brettanomyces, a yeast

The new laboratories at Bodegas Carrau.

Tasting booths in the laboratories.

that gives off-flavours in a wine, often wrongly blamed on the cork, and the commercial application of native non-Saccharomyces yeasts. Another interesting field, particularly for regular wine consumers, has been into the outstanding health benefits to be gained from drinking wines made from the Tannat grape! It seems that it contains just about everything that protects you against heart and a selection of other diseases. In such health conscious markets as the United States, surely this is a point to be stressed when promoting Uruguayan wines. All this research has been carried in conjunction with laboratories in California, Spain, France and Italy.

David Ramey, Paul Hobbs and Francisco Carrau at Chuck Hill winery in 1994. "Low input winemaking" strategies, inspiration for high quality wines in California.

In much of this work, Francisco has been greatly assisted by winemaker Octavio Gioia, who joined the company in 1988. His father's family has its roots in Piemonte and his mother's in the Veneto, so he comes from good wine stock. He studied oenology at university in Turin and is now responsible for production and quality control. His particular interests are in red wines made from Merlot and Cabernet.

This research has been of particular use in the developments of the new vineyards and wineries in Cerro Chapeu and across the border in Brazil, which are seen as being models of low-input winemaking.

The work that the Carraus have done has been recognised not just by the support that they have received from the Uruguayan and Brazilian governments, but also by a number of international awards. In 1992, they were the only wine company to receive an award for innovation from the Iberoamerican Cooperation Institute, for outstanding achievement in their field, in the celebrations to mark the five hundred years since the discovery of the Americas by Columbus, In 2001, they became one of the first wineries in South America to achieve ISO 9002:1994 and in the following year they achieved 2000 status. The brothers have also acted as consultants to nascent wine-industries in other countries, with Javier helping out in China in 1992 and Francisco in Bolivia in 1997.

Octavio Gioia – with Francisco, the heart of the winemaking team.

Another way in which the quality of the wines has been recognised and also of the potential of Uruguay as a country for fine wine production, is that on two occasions they have been sought out by important international wine producers as joint venture partners. The first, established with J. & F. Lurton, the Bordeaux-based brothers, in 1998, produced a red wine Casa Luntro. The children of this marriage were some great bottles of wine from the 1997 to 2000 vintages and these are much sought out by local connoisseurs.

The second is with the major Spanish company Freixenet and this has proved more long-lasting. The objective was to pool together the technical expertise of the Ferrer family in Spain and that of the Carraus. Together they created Viticultores del Uruguay S.A. in the year 2000. This owns 35 hectares of vineyards planted with Tannat, Sauvignon Blanc and Chardonnay. They also have access to the fruit of a further forty hectares belonging to three other growers. Originally it was thought that the result of this partnership might be a sparkling wine, but so far, the only offspring of the union to have appeared on the market is Arerunguá, an up-market barrel-aged Tannat. This means "just arrived" in the Charrúa language and takes its name from a piece of land given to the Uruguayan hero, General Artigas, during the revolution against the Portuguese in the north of the country. This was where the general made a treaty with the last of the native Charrúa to drive out the Portuguese.

The Carrau family realise that the customer, and even the potential customer, is all-important and attempt to draw him, or her, into the company, and its products, in every way possible. At the beginning of each school year, Tuesdays are set aside for the senior classes of primary schools, who are invited to learn about wine. Julia Martinez, who for many years was in charge of the bottling-hall, takes them round the winery and explains the various processes in wine-making to them. At the end of the tour, they are given a glass of grape juice and then set free to play football in the company park. The visit is backed up by an explanatory booklet, featuring an animated grape called Uvita, which includes a basic explanation of the background to wine and the company, a very short wine dictionary and some puzzles. Thus the local children learn to respect wine from an early age.

Julia Martinez with a school party.

(Despite her theoretical retirement, Julia is brought in to cook when any one is lunching at the winery and also acts as housekeeper at Cerro Chapeu. Her speciality is *torta frita*. The drive from there to Montevideo is a long one, but if she is on board, you can rest assured that the in-flight food service is first-class!)

As has been said the southern vineyards of the company are at Las Violetas, some 30 kilometres from the offices. However, a few rows of vines have been planted in Colón, just behind the winery. This means that visitors can be given some practical hands-on experience of working in the vines at such occasions as the *Festival de la poda y la cocina criolla* (The Festival of pruning and Creole cookery), the *Festival de la Vendimia* (Vintage Festival) and the Festival del Tannat y *el cordero* (The Festival of Tannat and lamb.). Some American tourists off a cruise ship were rather surprised to be given a pair of secateurs and a basket, and told to go out and pick grapes!

Since 1991, the Carraus have created around their wines an ever-expanding world of information aimed at advancing the knowledge and appreciation of their customers. This includes the magazine Vino y Crianza, newsletters, wine clubs, concerts, cookery events and tastings.

An amusing, but rather bizarre, story occurred in 2007 when, one day an elderly lady arrived at the offices, with her husband, clutching a little casket to her chest. She had rung in advance to see if she could speak to a member of the Carrau family, and Margarita was there to receive her. She explained that it contained the ashes of her father who had recently passed away and that his last wish was that they should be sprinkled in the Carrau vineyards, for he had drunk a bottle of Castel Pujol wine every day for the past 30 years. It was explained to her that the vineyards that

The Vintage Festival

The Tannat and Lamb Festival

The Wine & Art Festival

The Pruning
Festival

Music in the Cellar. 26 Concerts: Scantily Plaid, Carlos Nuñez , José Beledo and more.

produced the Castel Pujol wines were in the Las Violetas region some 30 kilometres away. Would she like them to sprinkle the ashes there? She replied that she was quite happy to have them scattered in any Carrau vineyards. Seeing the rows of vines alongside the winery, she said, "If you make wines from these vines here at the winery, this is the perfect place!"

Margarita Carrau is responsible for visits to the winery, as well as for oeno-tourism on a national scale, and she sees the ever-increasing number of cruise boats calling in at Montevideo as a useful way of introducing Uruguayan wines to the international consumer. Whilst they do not purchase much at the time of their visit, their memory should be jogged when they see Carrau wine on a shelf in their home country. The winery is fortunate in being only a short drive away from the port.

On the national field, one of Margarita's achievements has been the creation of Los Caminos del Vino, which groups together fifteen family wine companies on sixteen different locations, which open their wineries to visitors. Whilst the majority of these are within forty kilometres of Montevideo, others are further afield. There is also a map to locate them and details of what they can offer. As far as Carrau is concerned, in Colón this is tasting facilities, a wine boutique and food, whilst in Cerro Chapeu, accommodation is a further possibility. It is stressed however that, in both cases, advance notice of your visit is needed.

National Patrimony Weekend, at the end of October, is something dreamed up by the government as a sort of 21st century equivalent of bread and circuses. Companies are encouraged to throw open their doors to the general public and show them what they produce. Over the weekend Carrau might be host to 1000 visitors who come to taste and

The building for receiving visitors.

The original 19th century cellar.

The bottle fermentation cellar.

Oenoturism with Margarita at Bodegas Carrau

drink the wines and enjoy a monster barbecue. Currently, the winery receives over five thousand visitors a year.

Throughout the year, there is a programme of concerts and tastings. Margarita and Francisco also give lectures to sommeliers at the university.

In all, the company produces approaching 750,000 bottles a year and they are spread over almost 30 different products. At the entry level on the domestic market come three wines under the Casa de Varzi label, honouring the origins of the winery in Colón, where the wine pioneer established the country's first co-operative cellar. The first wine is a Uruguayan classic – a Muscat Rosé, made from a blend of Muscat Miel (very old vines of Muscat Giallo) and Merlot grapes. We have already seen how important rosé wine is on the domestic market and it is wines of this style that are most widely drunk. The other two wines at this level is a soft Tannat-Merlot blend that has seen no barrel treatment and a Chardonnay from vineyards in Las Violetas.

Next in the price-range come two separate teams of products called Castel Pujol. This brand was first launched in 1975 when the company started and the name reflects the family's Catalan origins. Castel is castle in Catalan and Pujol was the family name of Juan Carrau's mother, Catalina Pujol. The first team comes in the Franken *bocksbeutel* bottle, in a variety of sizes, and appears to be everywhere in the country's restaurants. It comprises a straight Tannat, a Tinto, a blend of Merlot and Cabernet Sauvignon, aged in bottle for six months before release, a Blanco blend of Sauvignon Blanc and Trebbiano and a Rosado, made from the same grapes as the Tinto. In parallel to this comes the Castel Pujol Altos and Robles team, in a traditional Bordeaux bottle. Here we have a Tannat-Merlot blend and a Cabernet Sauvignon. The main source for the grapes for the wines at this level is the vineyards at Las Violetas.

Again at the next level, Juan Carrau, we have two ranges of wines, the Cepas Nobles (Noble Vines) and the Reservas. The former comprises five different varietal wines: A Tannat, which has spent twelve months in American oak, a Cabernet Sauvignon, a Merlot, a Sauvignon Blanc and an unoaked Chardonnay. (I recently tasted the 1997 vintage of this wine and it still showed remarkable freshness, despite its age.)

It is at the Reserva level that true distinctiveness in the wines appears, for it was with wines such as these that the company was a true innovator. The Chardonnay is barrel-fermented in French oak, spends a further six months in cask and a further six months in bottle before it is released. The Sauvignon Blanc is fermented at low temperature (13°) and left on its lees for six months before bottling. It has an appealing zippy freshness. The Tannat Rosé, made from grapes from Las Violetas, is again fermented at low temperature, and made by the classic *saignée* method, before being bottled young to maintain maximal fruit flavours. The Pinot

Noir, and this is not a common variety in Uruguay, is aged for six months in new French oak and, whilst not being in a Burgundian style, has true varietal character. The Merlot is intense and rich, having spent ten months in oak, and the Cabernet Sauvignon, made from Cerro Chapeu fruit aged in French oak, is robust and full of flavour.

For fun eating, and a surfeit of red meat, the place to go in Montevideo is the Mercado del Puerto at the heart of the old city. Not long ago, at the Cabaña Veronica, one of the host of specialist parilla restaurants there, I enjoyed an eight-year-old bottle of the Tannat Reserva. One could not ask for a better accompaniment to a *baby bife*!

Rising even higher in the quality, and price, scale, one comes to the Grandes Reservas wines. There are four of these and, perhaps not surprisingly, all of them are red. Firstly, there is what is perhaps my favourite wine of the whole range, the 1752 Gran Tradición J.Carrau Pujol. This was first produced in the 1989 vintage. I was fortunate enough to taste, or rather, drink this recently at Panini's Restaurant in Montevideo and it is a wine that is still showing outstandingly, more than twenty years after its debut. It is made solely from Cerro Chapeu fruit; a blend of Tannat, Cabernet Sauvignon, Cabernet Franc and Merlot grapes. The wine is aged in new French oak for 18 months and a further year in bottle before release.

The name of Ysern Cabernet-Cabernet recalls Margarita Ysern who married one of the family ancestors Jaime Carrau in 1680. This wine is a marriage of the best Cabernet Sauvignon grapes from their two vineyards in Cerro Chapeu and Las Violetas; currently, the proportion is 60% of the former and 40% of the latter. The wine is aged for 18 months in second use French oak.

When Juan Carrau Sust first arrived in the country in 1930, he, and his Passadore and Mutio partners in Santa Rosa, planted the vineyard at Las Violetas. Within the plot that he personally planted was a hectare of what he believed to be Nebbiolo vines. It has recently been discovered that there are actually amongst them some of another historic Italian variety, the Marzemino. Also found were some very old vines of the Douro variety, the Sousao. In honour of his home town in Catalunya, he called this plot Vilasar. When the family reconstituted the vineyard in the seventies, they left alone these vines, which are now amongst the oldest in the country. They have a very low yield and produce a Nebbiolo, great enough to win prizes in competition with the best wines from its native Piemonte.

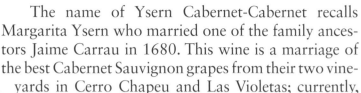

To celebrate the 260th anniversary in April, a second wine will be released under the Vilasar label. This will be a 2004 vintage Sousao, which will have spent more than two years in cask and five in bottle before it comes on the market.

The last wine in the range, Vivent, is

something rather different, a licor de Tannat. This is produced, in the Port manner, from ultra-ripe Tannat grapes from Cerro Chapeu. Grape spirit is added to the juice before fermentation has been completed. This kills the yeasts and leaves a considerable amount of sugar in the resultant wine. This is aged on its lees for 18 months, drawn off and bottled without filtration.

Mention has already been made of Arerunguá, the wine produced jointly with Freixenet, the Spanish Cava producer. The final still wine in the Carrau portfolio is their icon Tannat, Amat, named in memory of Eulalia Amat, the 18th century wife of Lorenzo Carrau . This wine is produced only in outstanding years from the best Tannat grapes from a single plot of vines, called Amat, at Cerro Chapeu. The wine is aged for 20 months, half in American oak and half in French. Some measure of the quality of this wine is the fact that the 2002 vintage is the only Uruguayan wine to feature in Neil Beckett's book, 1001 Wines to Taste Before you Die. I would prefer that you should drink it, rather than just taste it!

With Juan Carrau Sust's training in Vilafranca del Penedés, and his introduction of sparkling wines to the Uruguayan market with Santa Rosa, it is only fitting that they should feature in the current Carrau range. These are made solely by the bottle-fermentation method, with hand-riddling taking place in a dedicated cellar at Colón. Xacrat comes either as a Brut or a Demi-sec, is 100% Chardonnay and spends a minimum of twelve months on its lees. The superior quality Sust Vintage is a 70% Chardonnay/ 30% Pinot Noir blend and spends a minimum of

two years on its lees and also has zero dosage. These can be ranked amongst the outstanding sparkling wines of South America.

Whilst these wines just about complete the current range that the company offers, there have been others in the past, at least one that is about to be launched and others just on the drawing board! In the first category there used to be a sweet wine made from Muscat Miel; in the second there is an upmarket white wine under the 1752 Gran Tradición label, a blend of Petit Manseng (a variety like the Tannat  that has its roots in the foothills of the Pyrenees) and Sauvignon Gris and, just I am writing this, I receive a message about the successful launch of a Petit Verdot through the Norwegian State Monopoly. As for the more distant future, I would like to see a Cabernet Franc varietal wine, though there is a multitude of possibilities with the selection of varieties that is now being grown at Cerro Chapeu.

Bodegas Carrau is very much a Uruguayan company, but, in no way is it inward-looking. Already selling in more than 20 countries it is seeking to expand on export markets, because the domestic market, whilst being very solid, has limited possibilities for growth. However, why sell just Uruguayan wines? They have an answer to that question too, as we shall see in the next chapter.

CHAPTER VII

Across another road.

Rivera to Santana do Livramento.

An aerial view of the vineyards at Cerro Chapeu. The zig-zag road at the top of the picture marks the boundary between Uruguay and Brazil.

The boundary between Uruguay and Brazil is not like one of those drawn by the empire-builders in Africa during the 19th century: a straight line drawn across a white space on the map. As has already been said, it meanders along the crest of the hilly range that separates the two countries. At one point, there is a jagged spur of Brazil that bites into the Carrau vineyards in Uruguay. It may be that this offended Javier and Francisco Carrau; it may just be that they wanted to recreate part of their father's dream, a winery producing the finest wines in Brazil. Probably it was a bit of all of those things, but they decided to create a wine estate across the rough road that ran between the two countries.

It took Javier almost three years' hard negotiation with the landowner to buy the 60 hectares of land, which had originally been a cattle-ranch, that he sought, with the deal finally being completed in 2005. The price was $US1300 a hectare, more than four times the price that he had paid 30 years previously for the adjoining land in Uruguay.

Here there is a vision that is distinct from that for Uruguay. Firstly the idea is to create just one icon wine; secondly, and this is more in the long-term, it is to create a venue that will attract not just wine-lovers but also those who love nature.

To satisfy the wine-lover, this one wine will be made, with a limited production, and the first harvest for this has already been gathered in. The aim is to produce a master-piece red wine that will reflect the diversity of the immigrants to both Uruguay and Brazil. It will be a blend of three grape varieties, the Tannat from France, the Sousão from Portugal and the Teroldego from Italy. (It is also interesting to note that the oldest vines that the Carrau family own in their Uruguayan vineyards are of these three varieties.)

Whilst the Tannat plays the starring role as far as Uruguayan wines are concerned, it is only in Madiran in the rest of the world that it plays anything more than a bit part. In Madiran its intrinsic astringency has to be softened by blending with Cabernet Franc, Sauvignon and Fer. In Uruguay, however, it manages to play a solo role without offending the palate and appears in a number of guises ranging from a soft, juicy carbonic maceration wine to full-bodied, port-style, wines. It is also frequently blended with other varieties. Whilst it arrived in Uruguay, as the Lorda, from Argentina, there is now little of it planted in that country. There are token plantings of it in Brazil, but it is not a variety that has created an international reputation for itself.

The same might be said of the Sousão. It is very much a second division player in the Douro Valley, where it has largely been abandoned. Whilst it might form part of historical vineyards, it is very rarely planted nowadays. For example, there is some of it planted in the Noval vineyard but the resultant wine is generally not considered good enough to be included in the top-ranking Quinta do Noval blend. As Miles Edelman, from the Symington team of winemakers, says, "The grape has two major characteristics: massive acidity and good colour. It is also resistant to vineyard diseases."

Again, the Teroldego is scarcely in the forefront of grape varieties. It is very much a speciality of Trentino in northern Italy, so Francisco's collaboration with the research station there will be of great value. The grape is a relative of the Syrah and to produce successful wines it needs to have low yields. At their best these have spicy red fruit, deep colour, low tannins, but high acidity.

What is there about these three varieties that they

might, together, contribute to a great wine? If you look at their characteristics, it is not difficult to find there the constituents of the best red wines: fruit, tannin, acidity and colour. The artist will have enough colours on his palette to create the portrait; the winemaker has the ingredients, but he will have to get the best from each variety and then blend them together in the right proportions to obtain the ideal whole. One major advantage is that Francisco's many years of research into genetic plant material will mean that the most suitable clones of each variety should have been planted.

The objective is to produce no more than 60,000 bottles a year of premium wine, aimed primarily at the top end of the Brazilian domestic market. No name has yet been decided for the wine, but, given the precedent of the Uruguayan wines, regular use has been made of mothers' maiden names over the generations. Could this be the opportunity for Luigi Bonomi to be revived? Or that of his daughter Elena?

The winery has been built on the ridge that marks the boundary between the two countries; indeed it is less than 60 metres from the frontier itself. This gives it a dual vista; to the north over the Uruguayan vineyards, winery and guest-house and, to the south over the Brazilian Campanha, dominated by two striking examples of 'bowler-hat' hills.

In contrast to the octagonal shape of the winery over the border, the Brazilian one will be hexagonal. To take maximum advantage from its outlook, it will be topped by a mirador surrounded by a balcony, on the next floor down there will be a tasting-room, down yet again to a kitchen and laboratory, followed by the ground-floor above a subterranean cellar. This last will have four bays in the form of a goose-foot, three facing forwards and a shorter

February 2010 – Excavations begin.

July 2010 –

Construction of the underground cellars at the heart of the hexagon.

February 2011 - View from the heart of the cellar.

March 2011 – One of the wings is completed.

October 2011 – View of the cellar entrance with the stonework completed.

August 2010 - Blocks for the cellar ceiling.

December 2010 – The cellar is completed.

May 2011 – The other wing with new oak barrels containing the wine of the first vintage: 2011.

April 2011 – The first floor of the hexagonal tower.

June 2012 – The tower is finished with its double-brick walls.

The cellar door opens

The ground-floor plan for the Brazilan winery.

Santa Ana do Livramento.

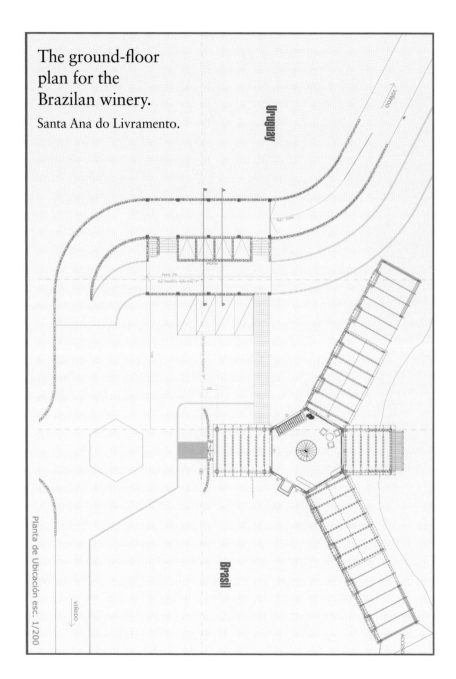

Uruguay

Brasil

Planta de Ubicación esc. 1/200

one facing back. (This design is based on the shape of the churches of the Knights Templar, where the longer central nave used to point towards Santiago de Compostela, the main mediaeval pilgrimage shrine in Europe. In this case, however, it will point northwards, in the direction of the major cities of Brazil – the potential market of the future!)

The site was originally covered with two types of trees: native forest and eucalyptus; this last has been widely planted in Uruguay as a cash crop. These latter have been cut down and the roots all removed. The native forest has been left alone and it is hoped that it will shortly form part of a nature trail, for it is home to a broad variety of birdlife. The land lies directly over the largest subterranean fresh-water aquifer in world – the Guaraní, which stretches down from Brazil and Paraguay.

Whilst there are already vines in production down the hillside, it is intended that up to three further hectares will be planted around the winery and, in the medium to long-term, it is hoped that a guest-house will be built and the whole site developed as a eco-friendly nature resort. Given the fact that it is only ten kilometres or so from two towns, each of which has a population of about 100,000 people and it has an airport even closer, when you are there, you have the impression of being in about as remote a corner of the world as possible. This will become an oenoresort with a difference, marrying together wine and nature.

There is no doubt that there is room on the Brazilian market for a red wine of this potential quality. It is a Holy Grail that the Carrau family has pursued since they first built Château Lacave more than 50 years ago. It has been pursued by Juan Luis Carrau with his Velho Museu wine, and there are now a number of other wineries in the country set out on the same trail. From those wines that I have tasted, I am not convinced that anything more than very good wines have been created; excellence is still there to be achieved. Here expense has not been spared to find the ideal site. The winery has been built to make the best wine and Francisco Carrau has already shown that he is capable of producing great wines. Perhaps here, by blending wines from these three unlikely grape varieties, he can create this masterpiece.

A natural spring surges from the ground in the native forest on the Brazilian estate

CHAPTER VIII

Where is the road leading to?

The company partners: Ignacio, Margarita, Javier, Gabriela y Francisco Carrau.

In 2010, there appeared a history of what had been the second largest Uruguayan wine company, Faraut written by Daniele Bonfanti and Mariana Viera Cherro. The title of one of the chapters can be translated as 'Are Wine Companies Immortal?' The answer in this case was a resounding, 'No!', for it had collapsed into bankruptcy in 1998. Amongst the problems that the authors considered responsible for this were: the involvement of too many members of the family in the company, excessive borrowings, a fall in consumption of their wines and problems with the unions. Could any, or all, of these influence the future of the Carrau family?

Let us look at these questions separately. Are there too many members of the family in the company? For sure, Juan Carrau had eight children, but in true Catalan tradition, they were encouraged to go out into the world to make their fortunes. Of the eight, three, Juan Luis, Elena and Inés, are no longer shareholders in the company and, of the five that are, only three could be said to be involved in the day to day affairs: Javier, Francisco and Margarita. Again, Francisco is also absent regularly in his role as head of the oenology department at the university and Margarita, too, works promoting oenotourism and Uruguayan wines in general. It could be said that Javier is the only one working full-time in the business.

Moving on to the next generation, the five shareholding members of the family have between them 13 children and three grandchildren, but, so far, only one, Marcos, Javier's son, has been directly involved in Bodegas Carrau, overseeing the vineyards at Las Violetas. However, currently, he has a scholarship to study for an MBA in Canada.

Interestingly, a major role in the immediate future has been identified for someone from this next generation: that of overseeing the two properties on the Uruguayan/Brazilian border. This will involve dealing with two sets of government, at all levels, developing the vineyards and the facilities on both sites and acting as host to the increasing number of trade visitors, now that accessibility is made more easy by regular commercial flights from both Montevideo and Porto Alegre to the airport on the doorstep. The sons and daughters were all invited to put their names forward for this post and four of them, all with differing qualifications, have done so. External consultants have been brought in to assess the merits of these applications and an appointment will be made on the basis of their recommendations. I think the family is wise to have encouraged in their children such a diversity of interests which can be utilised to best advantage either within, or outside, the family company.

The older part of the 10th generation – the future of the Carraus.

Any question of borrowing must be tied to Uruguay's overall financial position. The country has, in the past, been described as 'the Switzerland of South America', but, whilst it has, historically, like Switzerland, welcomed, under a certain cloak of anonymity, foreign money into the vaults of its banks, the Uruguayan peso has never enjoyed the same solid reputation as the Swiss franc. The main seekers of financial refuge have been the Argentines and the Brazilians, so the value of the peso has relied for its value too much on these neighbouring economies. Additionally, a major factor has been the credibility, or not, of the government in power in Montevideo. Certainly there was a frisson of fear for the future when José Mujica, was elected President as a representative of the Frente Amplio in 2010. His historical role as a Tupamaro guerrilla during the 70s gave many cause for concern. However, these concerns have been lessened by his appointment of Danilo Astori, a former successful finance minister, as his running-mate and, subsequently, Vice-President.

Whilst each country in South America has its individual currency, there is one that is all-powerful on the continent, and that is the US dollar. Because of this much financial dealing and trade is done in dollars. One of the major reasons for the downfall of the Faraut company was that it borrowed extensively, particularly in dollars, to finance the expansion of its business. Following the collapse of the Argentine economy under military rule in the early eighties, General Galtieri played his final ace, the nationalist card – and attacked the Falklands. This proved to be a disaster in financial as well as military terms. The value of the currency collapsed not only in Buenos Aires, but also in Montevideo. The comparative worth of the U.S. dollar soared and those who had borrowed heavily in that currency, found themselves perilously exposed. Such was the case with Faraut and it rapidly found its sources of credit cut off.

Yet again, in 2001, there was a financial crisis in Argentina and the government there imposed *el corralito*, limiting bank withdrawals to US$250 a week. However many canny Argentines had, in the meantime, deposited their money in dollar accounts in Uruguayan banks. With restrictions at home, they plundered their accounts abroad, withdrawing all their money. Within a matter of weeks Uruguay lost a third of its foreign reserves and five banks collapsed taking the Uruguayan peso, and many local companies with them. Inflation and unemployment soared and the country had to be saved by loans from the IMF.

All this meant nothing to Faraut, for they had not survived that long, but for other companies in the wine trade times proved to be very hard. As far as Bodegas Carrau was concerned, both in 1982 and 2002, they felt the pressure, but, because they had been very prudent in their borrowings, they were able to withstand it. With 40% of their sales on export markets and with their wines priced there in dollars, they do have a certain cushion. This cushion does, however, have two sides to it. If the value of the dollar goes too high, they have problems in competing on world markets.

Faraut suffered because of a decline in demand for their wines. Can the Carraus avoid this? Any answer to this must look at the question from three different aspects: global consumption of wine, and the company's position both on the domestic and export markets. As far as global trends are concerned, overall wine consumption appears to be falling. However, consumers are drinking better wines at the expense of cheaper everyday wines. As, from the moment that they established their own companies in Brazil and Uruguay, the family has studiously avoided the bottom end of the market (they have sold neither demijohns nor tetrapaks) they should, therefore, be able to face the global market with some confidence.

As for the domestic market, we have seen that the pressure of the arrival of Uruguay in Mercosur has led to a total restructuring of the vineyards, the grapes that they produce, and the wine industry as a whole. Part of this process was the creation of a sense of national pride in the wines produced in the country. It is interesting that if you visit a local supermarket, whilst there may well be a good range of Argentine and Chilean wines, pride of place is given to Uruguayan wines. Even more interesting is an almost total lack of European wines. In most other South American countries, as has already been mentioned, these are widely consumed as a mark of prestige.

With an average consumption within the country of 30 litres of wine a head, and, despite the changing nature of the wines available, that figure being maintained, it is not surprising that there is a certain optimism in the local wine industry. A small number of boutique wineries have been established over the past few years, producing wines for the top end of the market, and an Argentine investor is planting 200 hectares of vines, and building two wineries to cope with the output, near Maldonado.

Here again, the Carraus were far ahead of the field in the wines that they offer, and continuing investment in research and development has enabled them to maintain this position. They are by no means the biggest fine wine company on the market, but they are present in force both on the supermarket shelves and on restaurant wine-lists. The home market accounts for 60% of their business and their comprehensive distribution network enables them to maintain this presence.

With regard to exports, there are two separate markets as far as Uruguayan wines are concerned, Brazil and the rest of the world. I have already mentioned the difficulty that Brazil has in producing quality red wine. As a result, there is a vast demand for reasonably priced, quality red wine. Uruguay has been called upon to satisfy much of this demand.

If you look at the overall export sales figures for the country in, for example, the year 2007, they are dominated by one company, whose sales, in dollars, are almost four times that of the second name on the list. This company sells on just one export market. It is a Brazilian wine co-operative, based in the Serra Gaucha, which has established its own subsidiary in Uruguay. If you look at a bottle of this wine in Brazil, it is difficult to recognise it as being a wine made in Uruguay, for it appears dressed very much in the team colours of the Brazilian company. This might be described as commodity wine trading and is, as far as the Brazilians are concerned just a matter of price and convenience.

It must be to Brazil that Bodegas Carrau is looking for a substantial proportion of any future success, but at the opposite end of the market. Firstly it has substantial knowledge of and experience in the Brazilian market. It was involved in the earliest attempts to create a domestic fine wine industry there, firstly with Château Lacave, then with National Distillers and now with its own vineyards and winery, from where it is intended that smaller quantities of the full range of wines might be distributed when necessary. Secondly, it has a broad presence on the market through a dedicated sales-manager and two separate distribution networks and, finally, it has well-established members of the family living there; Ignacio and Gabriela have helped with sales there. Given that the potential market for wine in

Brazil would appear to be boundless, with increasing affluence and one of the largest populations in the world, there can be few companies in the industry that are better placed to succeed there.

However important the Brazilian market might become for the Carraus, it is also important that they do not neglect other world markets. Whilst I have some knowledge of many of these, I would like to look at one in particular; the British market. This I want to split into four different categories and see how capable Uruguay, and the Carraus, are of satisfying them. These categories are: commodity wines, fashion wines, restaurant wines and, finally, niche wines.

In the field of commodity wines, Uruguay is not well-placed (except, in the specific case of the Brazilian market). The vineyards, apart from one or two possible examples, are not big enough to have the economies of scale, or low enough labour costs, to compete with suppliers such as Australia, South Africa, Chile, Argentina and California. Nor do they have ideal climatic conditions. Furthermore there are not the financial resources, either from within the companies or provided by the government, to promote the wines on the same scale. Whilst Carrau have sold quantities of wine on two occasions to British supermarket chains, the buyers now seem unwilling to experiment with the wines they offer, relying rather on those suppliers who have big money to spend on promotion.

By fashion wines, I mean those wines, generally sold under the name of a grape variety, which, for whatever reason, become in demand. At present Pinot Grigio appears to be the wine on everybody's lips. Generally in Britain, there seems to be a trend to follow what has happened in America. We have drunk Lambrusco, Chardonnay, White Zinfandel and Merlot. Will Malbec be the flavour next month? In a bid to capture this market a number of New World countries have concentrated their sales efforts on one varietal, particularly one that is a speciality of their country. South Africa has promoted Pinotage, Chile, Carmenère and Argentina both Malbec and Torrontés. New Zealand created a distinct market sector for itself with Sauvignon Blanc and France, realising that its wine laws prevented it from being able to compete in this varietal market, has created the new level of wine, where this is possible, Vin de France.

One major problem with 'fashion' wines is if they become too fashionable too quickly. There is a limited acreage around the world of vineyards producing any one varietal and there are then inherent difficulties in producing more wine. It takes time for new plantings, or even graftings, to come into production and, by then, the fashion may have passed. One result is that fraudulent wine appears on the market in a bid to satisfy such demand, as we saw when sales of Pinot Noir increased in the United States by 45% in the year following the release of the film *Sideways*.

Whilst Uruguay has an individual grape in the Tannat, and we have already seen that it has featured this widely when promoting its wines, overall production is not adequate to satisfy large demand. To put things in perspective, one Chilean wine company produces more wine than the whole of Uruguay. Once again the production costs would make competing at this level difficult. Whilst I am sure that any Uruguayan wine company, including Bodegas Carrau, would welcome the opportunity to sell more wine, on a global scale their ambitions are, by necessity limited.

Many countries have a great gastronomic tradition and this leads to restaurants around the world offering their food and their wines to go with it. Thus, for example, in Japan, pasta is very popular and there is a significant number of

Italian restaurants to satisfy that demand. In turn, this means that there are significant imports of Italian wine to go with this food. To an even greater extent this is true of French cuisine and French wines. More surprisingly, there is in Britain a demand now for Indian wines for sale in the ubiquitous Indian restaurants, and Thai wines for Thai restaurants. Sadly, I know of no Uruguayan restaurants in Britain promoting the undoubted fleshly merits of the *parillada*, whilst there is a number of Brazilian and Argentine restaurants offering similar cuisine. The Gaucho Grill chain sells

Argentine wines; perhaps it does not realise that there are just as many gauchos in Uruguay and Brazil! Argentina, too, has appropriated the tango, when Uruguay can claim, with some sound evidence, that it is the country responsible for its creation – though in the spirit of reconciliation the dance has now been accepted as a joint patrimony of the two Río de la Plata capitals, Montevideo and Buenos Aires. If only there was an entrepreneur bold enough to launch a chain of Uruguayan beef and tango bars around the world, then Uruguayan wines would be introduced to the public on a global scale!

A tango performance at the Bodega.

Uruguay does have its unique musical tradition, the *candombe*, which goes back to African slave roots. The music is created by teams of drums, played with both sticks and the bare hand. The drummers are accompanied by exotically clad dancers. The best time to hear *candombe* is during the lengthy carnival season in February, though there is generally a troupe performing each weekend at the Mercado del Puerto. In homage to this tradition, the Carraus released a CD of *candombe* music in 2002.

Perhaps the niche market is the one to which Carrau wines are best adapted and it is here that they are meeting with some success. They are obtaining listings with the monopolies of both Canada and Scandinavia, but these need active agents to guarantee continuity of sales. In Poland, they have developed in another direction by working with a major wine club. Whilst Poland may not appear the most likely country for selling Uruguayan wine, it is one country in the European Union where the economy is thriving. This is reflected in rapidly increased demand for luxury goods and sales of table wines rose 7.1% in 2010 with double digit growth forecast for the future. Perhaps wine clubs are a potential field for sales in other countries. One has only to see the success of Laithwaites, now not just on the British market, but also in other countries such as France, Germany and Australia, to gain some idea of just what might be achieved. Such organisations are capable of moulding their customers' purchases to include wines from lesser known sources.

Creating a wine-brand around the world demands much investment, not just in monetary terms, but also man-hours. The team at Bodegas Carrau is not a large one, but is spreads its resources well, even though this involves regular absences maintaining a presence at the international wine fairs and working with importers.

One factor that caused serious problems not just for Faraut, but also for Santa Rosa, was that of industrial relations. Under left-wing governments the trade-unions began to flex their muscles and demand more and more from the employers. In the wine industry it was the larger companies that were the first to attract their attention. At Santa Rosa, for example this led to direct confrontations with management and a virtual lock-out, whilst at Bodegas Carrau, there was, and still is, much more of a family feeling in the workplace, with weekly meetings with the staff to discuss problems. For them the trade unions have posed no problems.

The Carrau team.

It is perhaps the size of the company that is its best guarantee for the future. Whilst it has expanded steadily, it has never overreached itself. As far as its products are concerned, it has pursued the path of quality, rather than quantity. To achieve this, it has been the leader in the country, both in the vineyards and in the wineries. It is fortunate that it has Francisco Carrau, ably supported by Octavio Gioia, with an international reputation in the field of research.

As far as sales are concerned, they have a solid base on the domestic market, with broad distribution both in the supermarket chains and in the restaurants. On their doorstep, they have the enormous potential of the Brazilian market. It is not by chance that the middle claw of their new goose-foot shaped winery points in that direction. It is there that they see a major part of their future and they are fortunate that they have a well-established track record in that country's wine-trade.

The family is fortunate, too, that it has a generation to succeed it that is qualified in a number of different directions. It is to be hoped that this is a generation that will continue along the path of putting into, rather than taking out of, the company. Over the centuries the Carraus, in the course of producing great wines, have crossed many roads. There can be no doubt that there will be many more similar challenges in the future.

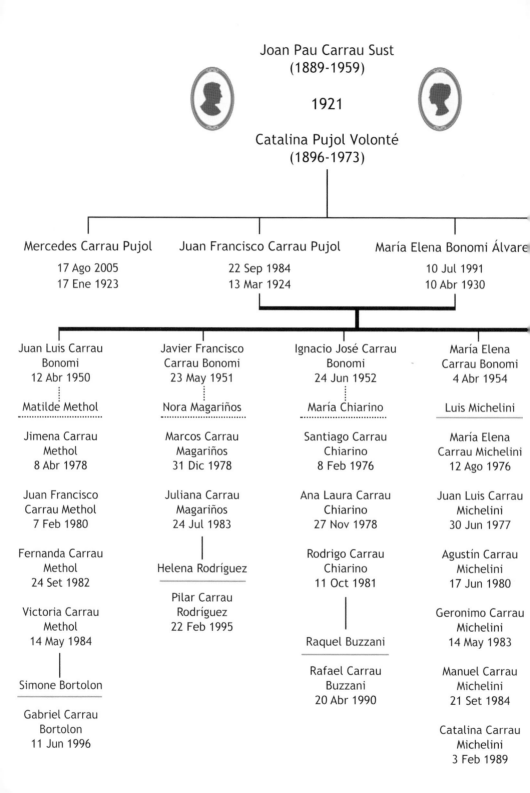

Joan Pau Carrau Sust
(1889-1959)

1921

Catalina Pujol Volonté
(1896-1973)

Mercedes Carrau Pujol
17 Ago 2005
17 Ene 1923

Juan Francisco Carrau Pujol
22 Sep 1984
13 Mar 1924

María Elena Bonomi Álvarez
10 Jul 1991
10 Abr 1930

Juan Luis Carrau Bonomi
12 Abr 1950

Matilde Methol

Jimena Carrau Methol
8 Abr 1978

Juan Francisco Carrau Methol
7 Feb 1980

Fernanda Carrau Methol
24 Set 1982

Victoria Carrau Methol
14 May 1984

Simone Bortolon

Gabriel Carrau Bortolon
11 Jun 1996

Javier Francisco Carrau Bonomi
23 May 1951

Nora Magariños

Marcos Carrau Magariños
31 Dic 1978

Juliana Carrau Magariños
24 Jul 1983

Helena Rodríguez

Pilar Carrau Rodríguez
22 Feb 1995

Ignacio José Carrau Bonomi
24 Jun 1952

María Chiarino

Santiago Carrau Chiarino
8 Feb 1976

Ana Laura Carrau Chiarino
27 Nov 1978

Rodrigo Carrau Chiarino
11 Oct 1981

Raquel Buzzani

Rafael Carrau Buzzani
20 Abr 1990

María Elena Carrau Bonomi
4 Abr 1954

Luis Michelini

María Elena Carrau Michelini
12 Ago 1976

Juan Luis Carrau Michelini
30 Jun 1977

Agustín Carrau Michelini
17 Jun 1980

Geronimo Carrau Michelini
14 May 1983

Manuel Carrau Michelini
21 Set 1984

Catalina Carrau Michelini
3 Feb 1989

The Carrau family
tree from 1930 onwards

María Elena Carrau Pujol	José Luis Carrau Pujol	María Rosa Carrau Pujol
25 Ago 1983	20 Nov 2001	
23 Ago 1925	13 Oct 1926	30 Set 1929
Horacio Leaniz	Elena Pellegrino	Horacio Campos

Gabriela Carrau Bonomi	María Inés Carrau Bonomi	Francisco Miguel Carrau Bonomi	Margarita Carrau Bonomi
3 Jul 1956	23 Jul 1959	15 Oct 1961	5 Oct 1966
Daniel Basile	Horacio Cervieri	Joyce Stewart	Renzo Ciceri
Piero Basile Carrau	Emiliano Cervieri Carrau	María Pía Carrau Stewart	Lucas Ciceri Carrau
14 May 1982	22 Set 1989	12 Ene 1987	25 Dic 1994
Martina Gabriela Basile Carrau	Valentín Cervieri Carrau	Cecilia Carrau Stewart	Tomás Ciceri Carrau
30 Ago 1984	4 Set 1991	24 Jul 1989	12 Ago 1996
	Carolina Cervieri Carrau	Felipe Carrau Stewart	
	3 Mar 1995	6 Jul 1995	

Vineyard Plantings
APPENDIX I

CERRO CHAPEU – total hectares 45

PRINCIPAL VARIETIES .... AGE .... HECTARES

Sauvignon Blanc.........................20 years 4
Tannat.................................5 a 33 years 10
Cabernet Sauvignon ....20 a 30 years 7
Pinot Noir ....21 years 2
Monastrell.............................7 years 1
Chardonnay ....12 a 33 years 3

CERRO CHAPEU SANTANA DO LIVRAMENTO– total hectares 5

PRINCIPAL VARIETIES .... AGE .... HECTARES

Souzao   ....6 years 1
Tannat..................................6 years 2
Teroldego ....6 years 1
Alvarinho ....1 years 1

LAS VIOLETAS – total hectares 44

PRINCIPAL VARIETIES .... AGE .... HECTARES

Merlot...................................14 a 20 years 10
Tannat.................................. 5 a 80 years 8
Cabernet Franc...........................16 years 3
Petit Verdot ....6 a 12 years 2
Nebbiolo .... more than 80 years 0.5
Souzao o Vinhao ....more than 80 years 0.5
Chardonnay ....12 a 33 years 6

A highly influential community of Catalans in Uruguay

by THOMAS HARRINGTON

APPENDIX II

All nations are held together, in one degree or another, by the phrases and anecdotes its citizens learn together while children in school.

Uruguay is no exception.

If you ask a Uruguayan to characterize the terrain of his or her country, it won't be long before the term "ligeramente ondulada" (gently rolling), a staple phrase of textbooks going back to the beginning of the 20th century, will find its way into the description.

Similarly, when you inquire about the country's first European settlers, you will hear with surprising consistency how that first group of pioneers--and from there, the early ethnic template of the nation-- was formed by Basques, Galicians, Canary Islanders as well as a smattering of *criollos* from across the river in Buenos Aires.

But while the description concerning the nature of the topography is undeniably accurate, the one about the country's ethnic origins falls somewhat short of the mark. Yes, it is true that settlers from the three territories of the Iberian periphery mentioned above were all there in sizable numbers.

But what is almost never noted is that they were accompanied from their earliest moments on the eastern shore of the River Plate by a compact but highly influential community of Catalans, people from the northeast corner of Spain (and parts of France), whose language, legal and familial traditions, commercial experience and overall levels of specialized education set them apart from Spain's other national/regional groups.

View of the walled city of Montevideo at the end of the eighteenth century.

Bruno Mauricio de Zabala, a Spanish officer of Basque descent, founded the Spanish fort overlooking Montevideo bay in 1724 in the hope of putting a brake on Portuguese ambitions in the region. A very short time later, he commanded one of his officers--Millan by name-- to begin distributing the fertile land lying along the bay's most important tributary to soldiers from the garrison.

According to the historian Isidoro de Maria, this area soon became known as the *Arroyo del Miguelete* (or Miguelete Stream) owing to the presence in that area of "a Spanish cavalry division known as Migueletes".

What the author of *Traditions and Memories of Old Montevideo* apparently did not know, however, was that the history of the Migueletes was firmly and indissolubly linked to Catalonia where, previous to their defeat at the hands of the Bourbon forces in the War of the Spanish Succesion in 1714, they had fought fierce and repeated battles against both France and Spain in the name of Catalan liberty.

Catalan conscripts as well as "volunteers"--after the imposition of Bourbon rule, the Migueletes fought for money as opposed to any devotion to the state--would remain an important element of colonial life over the next six decades. Regiments from Mallorca were a frequent presence in the city during the 1760s; in his famous *Guide for Blind Walkers from Buenos Aires to Lima*, published in the following decade, Carrió de la Vandera describes the Catalan mercenaries as filling the role of an elite defense force within the garrison.

But it was probably as a result of their role as teachers, doctors and construction engineers that the Catalans left their greatest mark on the first half-century of the city's existence.

Buildings designed by Catalan architects in Montevideo.

The colony's first educators were two Catalan Jesuits, Rafael Martorell and Cosme Agulló. They were followed by their countrymen Roch, Calabuig and Barchilon, the last of whom would provide the future Uruguayan President Oribe with his first lessons in reading and writing. And it was thanks to the generosity of the Valencian military officer cum trader Eusebio Vidal (like Mallorca, Menorca and Ibiza, that region was then considered an integral part of the Catalan speaking lands) and his wife, Clara Zabala, that the Uruguay's first school for women was founded.

The Catalan imprint on the life of the colony grew dramatically in the years immediately following 1778 when the Spanish government greatly expanded the number of Peninsular ports allowed to participate in the transatlantic trade. Before this, all Spanish commerce with the New World was required to be carried out through Seville.

Upon the passage of the new royal decree on trade, the Catalans, posessors of a millennial tradition of commerce within the Mediterranean, surged forth into the brave new world of the Atlantic. Within a few short years, Barcelona became the most dynamic and important of all Spanish ports.

And Catalan mariners and merchants became--thanks to their industriousness, their skill as navigators and ship-wrights and, perhaps most importantly, their dedication to a form of family-based capitalism which placed great emphasis advantageous marriage and calculated retention and distribution of wealth--the dominant commercial and social force in Havana, and from there, a number of other American cities.

A key turning point for the still embryonic community of Catalan traders in Montevideo, and quite arguably, the entire economic history of Uruguay, occurred in 1785 when a Catalan captain decided to fill the ship he had used to bring wines and finished products from Barcelona to Uruguay with salted meats for sale in Cuba.

According to José Manuel Pérez Castellanos, probably the most prestigious and wide-ranging chronicler Uruguayan colonial life, the Catalans were by 1787 the most important social force in Montevideo.

"Of all these projects rising up in the town, it can be said that *the Catalans are the yeast* because like good poor men they will do everything and be happy with whatever comes their way;…"

How commercially and socially dominant were the Catalans in Montevideo during the last 10 years of the 18th century and the first 15 years of the 19th century?

Those who have studied the period have probably come across names such as (and this is a very partial list), Batlle i Carreó, Illa, Salvañach, Juanicó, Costa i Teixidor, Bedell, Vilardebó, Carrera, Uset, Carafí, Brunet Carbonell, Ferrer, Pujol, Boix, Martí, Mateu, Font, Coll i Soler and Ferrés i Carrau.

Well, each and every one were Catalan.

The influence and power of the Catalans nucleus within the city and the region was so great, in fact, that they largely financed and organized the local defense against the British invasions of Buenos Aires in 1806 and Montevideo in 1807. They would do likewise when revolutionary elements from Buenos Aires sought, in 1810, to forcibly join Montevideo and its considerable wealth and power to their cause. Finally, they would act as the financial and strategic backbone of the city's defenses during the siege inflicted upon it from 1811 to 1814 by the *porteños*, and, intermittently, by soldiers loyal to José Gervasio Artigas, a Montevideo-born former Spanish military officer widely viewed today as a prime mover of Uruguayan independence.

During the decade and a half following the fall of Montevideo in June 1814, many of the Catalan merchants fled the Banda Oriental. They generally returned to Cuba or the Peninsula. However, a number of very important figures, such as Batlle, Vilardebó and Juanicó decamped to

Brazil. Gradually, however, most of the important members of the community returned to Montevideo.

A key moment in this process, as well as the overall maritime history of both Uruguay and Catalonia, occurred on January 10th, 1835, when a Catalan captain named Juan Mirambell piloted the schooner *Constancia* into Montevideo harbor.

Aware that Uruguay was still technically at war with Spain, he did so under a Brazilian flag. The ruse was soon uncovered and Mirambell was thrown into the brig as a prisoner of war. After five days in jail, he was brought before President Rivera. In his conversation with the Uruguayan leader he made clear-in a way that perhaps only a Catalan could-that his aims were purely commercial. Rivera, struck by his sincerity, not only exonerated him of all charges, but categorically lifted the existing ban on trade with the Peninsula.

And thus began the second great phase of Catalan influence in Uruguay. Over the next 25 years the espadrille-wearing seamen from the Peninsular northeast would largely re-establish their pre-eminent position within the port of Montevideo, and more broadly, the field of Uruguayan foreign trade. Wines, liquors and textiles would come from Barcelona. Once the ships were emptied in Uruguay, they would be filled with dried meats (from the *saladeros* of, among others, Pedro and José Ferrés i Carrau, both from Vilassar de Mar) the founder of the Carrau Trading Company the second son of the Vilassar-based wine producer Francisco Carrau Amat. There, the vessel would be filled with rum, or after a side trip to New Orleans or Savannah, with lumber, and eventually make its way back to the Catalan capital.

Like most mariners, Catalan seamen were expected to remain in the charge of their officers until otherwise notified. But often times, a disagreement with an officer or simply the dream of getting rich in the bustling economy they saw before their eyes, caused many of them to jump ship in the Uruguayan capital. One such person was Juan Carrau Ferrés, the founder of the Carrau Trading Company the second son of the wine producer Francisco Carrau Amat in Vilassar de Mar.

The latter half of the 19th century also saw a very important influx of Catalan educators to Uruguay. In 1926, an unnamed historian wrote:

"In past times, the term Catalan was a symbol of hard work, honor, art, culture, in short, it meant creative capacity. The truth of this assertion is evident in Uruguayan national life where there are thousands of examples that place the Catalan community on a solid pedestal. ... There are very few Uruguayans with college degrees or advanced studies that do not have something of the spirit of Cataluña in their souls because almost all of them have been taught by some at one time or another by a Catalan professor, teacher or grade school master."

Perhaps the most important of the early educational institutions founded or run by Catalans was the *Piarist School of Saint Philip and Saint James* established in 1835 by Pedro Giralt and 7 other Catalan Clerics (Sebastián Llobateras, Antonio Masramon, Ángel Singla, Fernando Cabañas, Joaquin Riba, Francisco Mata, and Marcelino Noriega Hoyos) in 1835.

The "Colegio de los Escolapios" as it was more commonly known, quickly became the school of choice for Montevideo's emerging social elite. Both José Pedro Varela, the father of the Uruguay's modern public education system, and José Batlle y Ordoñez, the great architect of its turn-of-the-century evolution into middle class society, studied there. It was also there that the theory and practice of stenography (whose first Spanish versions were generated in Barcelona) was introduced to Latin America by the Catalan Joaquim Pedralbes.

One precipitating factor in this flow of Catalan educators to Uruguay in the last third of the 19th were the political persecutions which followed the failure of the First Spanish Republic in 1874.

One of the people fleeing the crisis was Francisco Suñer y Capdevila who would go on to become, among many other things, one of the key promoters of Uruguayan Positivism, the first Dean of Medicine at the University of the Republic, and a founder of Montevideo's Spanish Hospital and Sanitorium.

Statue in honor of Enriqueta Compte y Riqué located in the Montevideo park named after José Enrique Rodó, himself son of a Catalan immigrant.

But perhaps the most influential of all of Uruguay's Catalan-born educators is Enriqueta Compte y Riqué, the woman who, in addition to founding Uruguay's (and Latin America's) first kindergarten, was a true pioneer in the fields of teacher training, educational psychology and the humane treatment of those suffering from alcoholism.

And given the focus of this book, there is probably one more late nineteenth century Catalan-born "scholar" we should mention. That is, of course, Francisco Vidiella.

Though he was self-taught and never occupied an official educational position, Vidiella greatly advanced the science of viticulture in Uruguay through his painstaking experiments aimed at matching grape varieties from all over Europe to local soils and climatic realities. Before the arrival of Juan Carrau Sust in the early 1930s, he was, along with the French Basque immigrant, Harriague, the person who most contributed to the professionalization of the country's wine industry.

THOMAS HARRINGTON is Associate Professor of Hispanic Studies at Trinity College in Hartford Connecticut where he teaches courses on 20th and 21st Century Spanish Cultural History, Literature and Film. His areas of research expertise include modern Iberian nationalist movements, Contemporary Catalonia, and the history of migration between the peninsular "periphery" (Catalonia, Galicia, Portugal and the Basque Country) and the societies of the Caribbean and the Southern Cone.

In addition to his work in Hispanic Studies, Harrington is a frequent commentator on political and cultural affairs in the US and abroad.

A.

B.

C.

The Carrau Family in Generational Order.

Carrau, Juan (1651), 13-14.

Carrau Pau (1730), 17.

Carrau Vehils, Francisco (1752), 17-18.

Carrau Mir, Francisco (d 1775), 18, 19, 30 32, 35, 36,45.
Carrau Mir, Jaume, 18.

Carrau Girbau, Lorenzo (d. 1810), 18.
Carrau Girbau, Magí, 19.

Carrau Amat, Francisco (b. 1796), 18, 184.

Carrau Ferrés, Juan (1823- 1897), 9, 24, 25, 26, 30-35, 185.
Carrau Ferrés, Lorenzo (d. 1856), 27.
Carrau Ferrés, Pablo, 28-29.
Carrau Ferrés, José, 28.
Carrau, Pedro, 27.

Carrau Mir, Francisco (1860-1902), 18, 19, 30, 32, 35, 36, 45.
Carrau Mir, Jaume, 18.
Carrau, Francisco (son of Pedro), 29-30

Carrau Sust, Juan (b. 1890), 13, 16, 30, 36, 40, 45, 50, 56ff. 97, 148
Carrau Sust, Josefa, 16.
Carrau Sust, Francisco, 70.

Carrau Pujol, Juan (Quico), 40, 68ff, 75ff, 79ff, 103ff, 113ff, 135.
Carrau Pujol, Mercedes, 66.
Carrau Ochoa, Julio, 88.

Carrau Bonomi Juan Luis, 76, 91-93, 159.
Carrau Bonomi, Javier, 8, 76, 85-86, 87, 114ff, 131, 134 135, 138, 153, 174.
Carrau Bonomi, Ignacio, 94, 95.
Carrau Bonomi, Gabriela, 94, 95.
Carrau Bonomi, Inés, 94.
Carrau Bonomi, Elena, 94.
Carrau Bonomi, Francisco, 116, 117, 134, 138, 155, 160.

D.

E.

F.

G.

H.

I.

J.

K.

L.

M.

N.

O.

P.

Q.

R.

INDEX